Making the Classroom Work for Every Child

Every learner, no matter their starting points or backgrounds, and no matter their additional and different needs, should have a fair and equitable chance of succeeding at school. This second book in the Equity in Education series explores ways of making the curriculum, teaching, and assessment more inclusive of every child.

It considers the reasonable adjustments teachers can make to support children with additional and different needs, and it examines the role oracy and reading for pleasure can play in 'levelling the playing field' for disadvantaged learners in helping them compete equitably with their peers. Providing a practical roadmap to ensure lesson planning, teaching strategies, and assessment methods are inclusive of every child, the chapters cover:

- Inclusive curriculum planning
- Talking to students' lived experiences
- Adaptive teaching and reasonable adjustments
- Assistive technologies
- Attainment gaps including those caused by gender, ethnicity, SEND, socio-economic deprivation, mobility, and being in care
- Belonging and well-being
- Oracy and reading for pleasure

Offering actionable guidance and strategies, the book sets out the practical ways teachers can create a classroom environment where all students can thrive. As such, it is essential reading for all teachers and school leaders who want to give every child an equitable chance of success at school and in later life.

Matt Bromley is CEO of *bee* and Chair of the *Building Equity in Education Campaign*. He is an education journalist, author, and advisor with over 25 years' experience in teaching and leadership including as a secondary school headteacher and academy principal, further education college vice principal, and multi-academy trust director. He is a public speaker, trainer, initial teacher training lecturer, and school improvement advisor. He remains a practising teacher, currently working in secondary, FE, and HE settings. Matt writes for various education magazines including *SecEd* and *Headteacher Update*, and he is a columnist on *The Yorkshire Post*. He is the author of numerous best-selling books on education, and he co-hosts an award-winning podcast.

Equity in Education Series
Series Editor: Matt Bromley

Schools sometimes fail to talk to the lived experiences of disadvantaged and vulnerable children, as well as those with additional and different needs – and, because they do not feel included in the school's social and emotional environment and the academic curriculum, they do not feel it is for them. This exciting new series looks at how schools can remove barriers to belonging and ensure they include the excluded and mitigate the effects of an unequal, fractured society. The books offer strategies to help schools foster a whole-school ethos of equity and inclusion, tackle the many causes of disadvantage, foster a sense of belonging for all, plan an ambitious curriculum that's accessible to all, and prepare learners for future success.

Why School Doesn't Work for Every Child
How to Create a Culture of Inclusion and Belonging
Matt Bromley

Making the Classroom Work for Every Child
How to Plan, Teach, and Assess Inclusively
Matt Bromley

For more information about this series, please visit: Equity in Education Series – Book Series – Routledge & CRC Press

"In the second book in the Equity in Education series, Matt Bromley extends and deepens his discussion of inclusion in education across all aspects of this vital concept. Accessible, practical and rooted in schools and classrooms, *Making the Classroom Work for Every Child* is an excellent "how to" guide for every teacher looking to make their classroom more inclusive."
– **Chris Hildrew**, Headteacher at Churchill Academy & Sixth Form

"*Why School Doesn't Work for Every Child* is the clarion call that our education system needs if we are to finally overcome the consequences of disadvantage and inequality that too many children and young people face. As we have come to expect, Matt Bromley offers insightful and practical advice for schools and educators striving to make a difference for their students from disadvantaged backgrounds. His ability to distill complex educational concepts into actionable strategies makes his writing a valuable resource for teachers and school leaders at all levels. This is why he is one of SecEd's most prolific and popular authors. His ideas are grounded in real-world classroom experience, making them both relevant to the challenges schools are facing today and easily adaptable and actionable for your school's context. Matt Bromley has become one of the most relevant, useful and inspiring voices in education – and this book is no exception."
– **Pete Henshaw**, Editor for SecEd and Headteacher Update magazines

"I love this book!!!
This book focuses on the hugely complex issues of equity and inclusion, with a real razor sharp focus on the causes and consequences of what it is to be a disadvantaged student. Where Matt gets it right is to focus on practical and simple solutions and he keeps the focus tight, honing in on the importance of attendance, positive behaviour and generating a community. If you want a book that is brimming with practical advice, hints, tips and guidance from someone who actually does the job then this is the book for you. The secret is the author keeps it real!
What a gem of a read. Bravo!"
– **Sam Strickland**, Principal and CEO

"Matt's book series is a timely collection for UK based educators looking to level the playing field for disadvantaged students and 'build more equity in education'. Matt's ABC framework provides a meaningful reference point to help cut through the complexities required to create an inclusive school culture. In addition, his framework will help schools to unpick institutional factors that prevent students from attending school. No matter your stance in education, this book series is essential reading."
– **Bukky Yusuf**, Leadership Coach

"Rooted in the realities of children's lives, this book from master story-teller Matt Bromley will prove invaluable in helping school leaders ask themselves hard but essential questions about equity and inclusion."
– **Jean Gross CBE,** former government Communication Champion for children

"In this essential first volume of the *Equity in Education* series, Matt Bromley confronts one of today's most pressing challenges: building a culture of true inclusion and belonging in schools. With a fresh look at educational disadvantage and the widening societal divide, Bromley offers practical, research-backed strategies to create environments where every student can thrive. Anchored in real-world school experience, the book's straightforward ABC framework—Attendance, Behaviours, and Community—equips educators with actionable tools to address inequity head-on. This is more than a call for change; it's a guide for educators ready to make a meaningful impact and challenges the misconception that we can do this alone with high expectations and zero tolerance approaches in schools."
– **Sean Harris**, Director of People, Learning and Community Engagement, Tees Valley Education

"*Why School Doesn't Work for Every Child* neatly brings together the evidence and offers practical steps for those working on school priority areas such as attendance. This book reminds us to put learner and family experiences of school life at the forefront of our work, and to continuously reflect on our work on inclusion to ensure school works for every child."
– **Kate Anstey**, Director of Education, the Child Poverty Action Group

Making the Classroom Work for Every Child

How to Plan, Teach, and Assess Inclusively

Matt Bromley

LONDON AND NEW YORK

First published 2026
by Routledge
4 Park Square, Milton Park, Abingdon, Oxon OX14 4RN

and by Routledge
605 Third Avenue, New York, NY 10158

Routledge is an imprint of the Taylor & Francis Group, an informa business

© 2026 Matt Bromley

The right of Matt Bromley to be identified as author of this work has been asserted in accordance with sections 77 and 78 of the Copyright, Designs and Patents Act 1988.

All rights reserved. No part of this book may be reprinted or reproduced or utilised in any form or by any electronic, mechanical, or other means, now known or hereafter invented, including photocopying and recording, or in any information storage or retrieval system, without permission in writing from the publishers.

Trademark notice: Product or corporate names may be trademarks or registered trademarks, and are used only for identification and explanation without intent to infringe.

British Library Cataloguing-in-Publication Data
A catalogue record for this book is available from the British Library

ISBN: 978-1-041-11349-2 (hbk)
ISBN: 978-1-041-11348-5 (pbk)
ISBN: 978-1-003-65956-3 (ebk)

DOI: 10.4324/9781003659563

Typeset in Meridien
by Apex CoVantage, LLC

Contents

Series dedication and acknowledgements ix

Introduction 1

Part one: Equality, diversity, and inclusion

1 Thomas and Tommy 11

2 Equality, diversity, and inclusion 22

3 The 3Cs of inclusion 27

Part two: Mind the gaps

4 The gender gap 39

5 The ethnicity gap 46

6 The SEND gap 52

7 The socio-economic gap 58

8 The vulnerable children gap 64

9 The mobility gap 70

10 Other causes of difference and disadvantage 76

Part three: Inclusive planning, teaching, and assessment

11 Inclusive lesson planning　　　　　　　　　　　　87

12 Inclusive teaching　　　　　　　　　　　　　　　96

13 Inclusive assessment　　　　　　　　　　　　　104

14 The SEND system　　　　　　　　　　　　　　115

Part four: Oracy and reading for pleasure

15 Oracy and inclusion　　　　　　　　　　　　　125

16 Oracy – the road to equity　　　　　　　　　　134

17 Reading for pleasure　　　　　　　　　　　　　169

Part five: Putting it into practice

18 Action planning　　　　　　　　　　　　　　　187

　　Index　　　　　　　　　　　　　　　　　　　　199

Series dedication and acknowledgements

In this series, *Equity in Education*, I espouse the importance of putting families first so allow me to practice what I preach . . .

Firstly, I'd like to thank my wife, Kimberley, for her constant love and support. Thanks also to our children, Matilda, Amelia, and Harriet, and to my parents, Ray and Violet, and my in-laws, Dave and Karen.

I also argue in this series that it takes a village to raise a child and a community to educate one. This sentiment is true of writing a book, too. Although it can, at times, feel like a lonely pursuit, sitting solo at a computer trying – sometimes in vain – to populate a blank page, it is in fact a team sport. The words in this book may be my own, but the ideas behind them are far from it.

Secondly, therefore, I'd like to thank all the inspirational people – educators and academics, and parents and children – who I've worked with over the years, and whose words and actions have filled my cup, percolated there awhile, then filtered into my thoughts.

Thirdly, my thanks to all those colleagues who have freely given their time to read and comment on this book, and the previous book in this series, and offer kind words of encouragement and praise. Thanks, too, to everyone at Routledge who has helped deliver this book into your hands.

This series is about making schools more inclusive places by fostering a better sense of belonging. Book 1 explored whole-school culture; this book dives into the classroom and examines ways of making lesson planning, teaching, and assessment more inclusive of every child. It is about doing more for those who start with less so that a child's birth is not also their life's destiny.

And, therefore, my final dedication aptly goes to anyone who doesn't yet feel they belong and who doesn't yet know their place in the world. Whoever you are, wherever you come from: Hold on; be strong. Your time will come, and you *will* find your way in the world. Life is unfair, society is unequal. You may have started the race further behind most of your competitors, and you may not be wearing the right running shoes on your feet. But keep going because you will reach that white tape and complete the race. It may take you longer and the terrain may at times be tough but persevere and be proud of who you are and what you do. If you falter, look left and right. You are not alone. We are here. We have got you. And together, we will help each other over the finish line. We are your tribe, and you belong right here.

Introduction

About this series

Equity in the education system has never been more important. We live in an increasingly unequal, fractured society, and schools, as microcosms of that society, are becoming increasingly unequal, fractured institutions. Schools cannot solve all of society's ills, of course, and nor should they be expected to, but they can do more to ensure a child's birth is not also their destiny.

Currently, disadvantaged children – whether that be those living in poverty, those from underrepresented cultures, ethnicities, and backgrounds, those with transient lives, or those with special educational needs and disabilities – start school behind their peers and schools fail to close the gap. In fact, that gap widens as children travel through the education system, in part because knowledge begets knowledge: Those children who start out behind, find it harder than their peers to access the school curriculum and achieve, and thus they fall further and further behind.

Covid exacerbated the problem. There's been a marked rise in absenteeism since the pandemic and disadvantaged children are more than twice as likely to be persistently or severely absent as their peers, leading to lower progress, outcomes, life chances, and earnings power, not to mention poorer health and well-being. Disadvantaged children are more likely to experience mental health issues and struggle to study at home or access additional extra-curricular provision.

The school curriculum often fails to talk to disadvantaged children's *lived experiences* and, because they do not see themselves reflected in the school curriculum, they do not feel it is for them. Furthermore, they often lack the background knowledge and word power needed to access the full curriculum and so fail to achieve their potential.

It is not that these children are less able than their peers, nor that they do not exert the same amount of effort; it is the knowledge and skills gaps (what we might reductively call 'cultural capital') which result from their circumstances that pose a barrier to their success at school and then in later life.

This four-book series will explore ways of removing those barriers and providing a more equitable education to all; it will provide practical strategies to help schools *include* the *excluded* and mitigate some of the effects of an unequal, fractured society.

How the series is structured

Book 1 in the series looked at ways of improving the attendance of disadvantaged learners, as well as at ways of helping them to develop appropriate behaviours and attitudes to learning and life. Book 1 also explored the importance of working with parents and the local community to provide the best start in life for the most vulnerable children in society.

Book 2 – the one you're holding in your hands now – explores ways of making curriculum planning, teaching, and assessment more inclusive of every child, including by making reasonable adjustments so schools do not discriminate against children based on their additional and different needs. It also examines the role oracy and reading for pleasure can play in 'levelling the playing field' for disadvantaged learners and helping them compete equitably with their peers.

Book 3 will examine how to embed high expectations for all and ensure high challenge with low threat. It will explore the importance of language and literacy, including disciplinary literacy, and how to make a success of additional interventions. Book 3 will also consider how to use extracurricular provision to develop learners' cultural capital, as well as how to build intrinsic motivation through enrichment and employability.

Book 4 will explore ways of helping learners to become increasingly independent. It will look at ways of preparing disadvantaged learners for future success and examine how to teach metacognition and self-regulation, as well as study skills and revision strategies. Book 4 will also examine how to make marking and feedback more meaningful and motivating so that it expedites learners' progress and improves their outcomes.

About this book

This is the second book in the series – it is not necessary for you to have read Book 1 before reading on, as each book in the series stands alone – and it will explore ways of removing barriers to inclusion and belonging, and providing a more equitable education for all; it will provide practical strategies to help teachers *include* the *excluded* in their lessons and mitigate some of the effects of living in an unequal, fractured society.

Here's how it's structured . . .

Part one: Equality, diversity, and inclusion

Chapter 1: Thomas and Tommy

In Chapter 1, we revisit the two teenage boys we met in Book 1. They have now finished their GCSEs. Thomas, an affluent middle-class boy, is studying A Levels in the school sixth form; Tommy, who lives in poverty, failed to get the grades needed and is resitting English and maths at the local further education college. We explore their lives as case studies to demonstrate the impact that a child's homelife and circumstances can have on their ability to engage with school and succeed.

Chapter 2: Equality, diversity, and inclusion

This chapter defines the terms 'equality', 'diversity', and 'inclusion' and explores systemic barriers, social barriers, and practical barriers to achieving EDI. This chapter also examines ways of embedding EDI in policy and practice, empowering staff and learners, celebrating diversity, and prioritising well-being and accessibility. Further, it looks at school-based, home-based, and learner-based factors that can impede on inclusion and belonging.

Chapter 3: The 3Cs of inclusion

This chapter explores the 3Cs of inclusion: Culture, collaboration, and curriculum, and examines what this looks like in the classroom. It offers three features of an inclusive curriculum (reflect, reveal, and review), three features of inclusive teaching (diagnose, deliver, and differentiate), and three features of inclusive assessment (accessibility, adjustments, and assistive technologies).

Part two: Mind the gaps

In Part Two of the book, we'll explore various causes of attainment gaps in schools. The first six chapters in this section explore a different gap and include supporting data to show the scale of the gap and the extent to which it has changed over the last two decades. Each of these six chapters also offers a series of specific, practical solutions for addressing the gap. It's worth noting that some of the underlying causes are similar and so too are the solutions. You will, therefore, note some repetition between the chapters in this section of the book. However, it's important to acknowledge each gap separately so we do not conflate the issues or assume a 'one size fits all' approach. By exploring each gap individually, it will also be easier for colleagues to dive into the chapter which explores the gap that's most pertinent to their school context without the need for cross-referencing.

Chapter 4: The gender gap

Chapter 5: The ethnicity gap

Chapter 6: The SEND gap

Chapter 7: The socio-economic gap

Chapter 8: The vulnerable children gap

Chapter 9: The mobility gap

Chapter 10: Other causes of difference and disadvantage

The final chapter in this section explores school-based causes of attainment gaps including:

- Parental engagement and expectations
- School leadership and the quality of teaching
- School resources and infrastructure
- Teacher perceptions and biases
- Transition points
- Social and emotional well-being

Part three: Inclusive planning, teaching, and assessment

Chapter 11: Inclusive lesson planning

This chapter examines three ways of making the curriculum and lesson plans more inclusive of all learners: 1 Cross-curricular connections, 2 Classroom consistency, and 3 Connections to the real world.

It argues that the more meaning we can attach to the curriculum, making abstract information more concrete and real, connecting the new with the familiar, the more able learners will be to transfer that knowledge across domains. A part of this is finding connections across the school curriculum, enabling subject disciplines to talk to each other and complement each other.

It also argues that the more consistency there is in what we teach and how we teach it, the more able learners will be to access the curriculum and understand it. Consistency across subject disciplines – especially when teaching shared concepts or methods like mathematical techniques or essay-writing – offers significant advantages for learners and teachers alike. By aligning approaches, we provide clarity, reduce cognitive load, and ensure that learning is transferable.

This chapter also purports that, as teachers, we should also connect what we teach with the world beyond our school gates because using real-world examples in teaching is a powerful tool for making learning more relevant, engaging, and impactful. For disadvantaged learners, who may have fewer opportunities to experience certain cultural, social, or professional contexts, these examples also play a critical role in building cultural capital.

Chapter 12: Inclusive teaching

Whilst the whole book explores inclusive classroom practice, this chapter looks specifically at ways of ensuring lessons are inclusive of all learners, that every child can access the same ambitious curriculum and achieve their potential. It examines the difference between traditional differentiation and adaptive teaching and offers practical examples of using task-scaffolding to make the curriculum accessible to all. It explores live and planned adaptations, adapting the support, size, and style of learners' work, and addressing the four challenge variables (intrinsic demand, cognitive load, prior knowledge, and external support) by sequencing, adapting, activating, and scaffolding.

Chapter 13: Inclusive assessment

This chapter argues that assessments can be discriminatory because of cultural capital biases, language barriers, socio-economic disparities, SEND, gender stereotypes, and an overemphasis of one type of intelligence. It recommends diversifying assessment formats, providing adjustments for SEND learners, ensuring cultural relevance in assessment materials, reducing the role of high-stake testing, offering support for EAL learners, addressing socioeconomic barriers, challenging gender stereotypes, and involving learners in the process of designing assessments. It also offers practical advice on dealing with cultural capital biases in external assessments, handling differences in learners' prior knowledge, and helping learners to cope with the anxiety of high-stakes assessments.

Chapter 14: The SEND system

SEND runs through this book – and indeed the whole series – like the letters in a stick of rock. But this chapter offers a deep dive into the SEND system. It explores what *reasonable adjustments* might look like in practice and examines practical strategies for adapting lessons for cognition and learning needs, addressing communication and interaction needs, supporting social, emotional, and mental health needs, addressing physical and sensory needs, and embedding routines for success. It also takes an honest look at the SEND system and offers some systemic and school-based solutions to making it a success.

Part four: Oracy and reading for pleasure

Another dimension to inclusion, underpinning lesson planning, teaching, and assessment, is oracy – the power of spoken language and communication. After all, if belonging is about all learners feeling valued and respected and included, how can we achieve this if learners are unable to express themselves and have their voices heard?

In this series, we will also explore language and literacy more widely, including the importance of disciplinary literacy – the ability to speak, read, and write like subject specialists. But in this book, we start with oracy because a person's written language capabilities cannot exceed their spoken language capabilities. The spoken word must therefore come first.

Oracy refers to the ability to express oneself effectively and to understand spoken language in various contexts. It encompasses the skills required to communicate clearly, listen actively, and engage thoughtfully in dialogue. Oracy is as vital to education as literacy and numeracy, yet it is sometimes neglected in favour of these more traditional pillars. If we are to equip young people with the tools they need to succeed in life, we must place oracy at the heart of our classrooms. That's why there are two chapters dedicated to this important subject . . .

Chapter 15: Oracy and inclusion

This chapter explores why disadvantaged and vulnerable children may lack oracy skills and what schools can do about it. It offers a six-step plan for using oracy as a means of promoting inclusion.

Chapter 16: Oracy – the road to equity

Building on the previous chapter, this one argues that, if we are serious about addressing educational inequality, we must make oracy a central pillar of our teaching. Oracy is the road to equity. It argues that oracy is not just about language capability; it's about confidence, too. This chapter offers five practical strategies for using oracy as a road to equity:

1. Teach code-switching to enable learners to speak appropriately and with confidence in a range of situations

2. Teach debating skills to enable learners to engage in discussions and articulate their views with diplomacy

3. Teach rhetoric and prosody to enable learners to speak convincingly and powerfully to argue their views

4. Teach storytelling techniques to enable learners to narrate their own lives and the lives of others

5. Deploy dialogic teaching and modelling in the classroom to make oracy an integral part of the curriculum

Chapter 17: Reading for pleasure

Along with oracy, reading for pleasure is a key indicator of academic success and a powerful lever for achieving equity. Reading for pleasure is not merely a leisurely pastime; it is a cornerstone of lifelong learning and personal growth. Unlike the mandated reading tasks of school curriculums, where texts are often dissected for meaning and analysis, reading for pleasure invites an intrinsic, self-motivated engagement with stories, ideas, and knowledge. This distinction is crucial, for it is through this voluntary immersion that we unlock a host of benefits that extend far beyond the pages of a book.

This chapter argues that reading stories for pleasure is vital for helping all learners engage at school and in life and thus key to fostering a culture of inclusion and belonging. It explores practical ways of fostering a culture of reading for pleasure in schools, including by promoting reading among boys. It examines the link between reading for pleasure and language and literacy skills. And it explores the link between reading for pleasure and inclusion and belonging.

Part five: Putting it into practice

Chapter 18: Action planning

This chapter pulls all the advice contained in the book together and offers a seven-step process as well as an action plan for school leaders and teachers to use to turn the theory into practice in their schools and classrooms. This action plan, like the rest of the book, can be used in isolation, or it can be added to the action plan at the end of Book 1 to form a longer, more holistic plan for promoting equity.

A note on the text

Responsible inclusion is about making sure every child is educated in the most appropriate setting to meet their needs. Most children can and should be taught in the mainstream classroom. But for some, this would be discriminatory because some mainstream schools are not able to make the reasonable adjustments required to support a child with more significant needs, either due to deficits of money or expertise, or logistical barriers such as limitations with regards to physical facilities and accessibility.

In this book, I'm focusing on what we can do within the mainstream classroom to achieve inclusion and belonging. But I acknowledge that, for some, specialised provision in a different setting, or access to an alternative curriculum, is needed.

A further note: I use the term 'disadvantage' in this book, but I know some people find this problematic, in part because of its pejorative nature. It's increasingly common to refer to those who live in poverty as 'under-resourced' rather than disadvantaged, and, whilst this word is also far from perfect, I agree it's more accurate and less derogatory. However, in this book, as in the whole series, I'm exploring the myriad reasons why a child might be disadvantaged at school, whether that's because they are under-resourced, live in care, have transient or unpredictable lifestyles, belong to certain cultures or ethnicities, or have special educational needs or disabilities. I will continue to use the term 'disadvantaged', therefore, to capture the fact that some young people face greater challenges at school than others.

PART ONE
Equality, diversity, and inclusion

1 Thomas and Tommy

Figure 1.1 Image – Thomas and Tommy © Getty Images

The story so far

In Book 1 in this series, we met Thomas and Tommy, two 15-year-old boys. I'd visited them at home whilst they were both in Year 11 studying for their GCSEs.

Thomas lived with his mum and dad in a five-bedroomed detached house in leafy suburbia. There was a large, manicured garden, home cinema, a study with more

DOI: 10.4324/9781003659563-3

books lining the walls than the local library, and a heated swimming pool in the basement.

Until recently, Tommy had lived with his mum and dad, but he and his mum were taken into emergency accommodation. Their temporary flat was on the other side of town. It had one bedroom and one reception room. The reception consisted of a kitchenette and a threadbare sofa which was more spring than cushion. There was a shared bathroom down the corridor which didn't have a lock on the door or a shower over the bath. The carpets were sticky and the whole building smelled of damp. Tommy shared the bedroom, top-and-tailing with his younger sister; his mum took the sofa. The ceiling leaked and the incessant drip-drip was distracting, like a head full of bees. The heating system was on the blink, but Tommy's mum couldn't afford the heating bills anyway.

Thomas had quite the social life: Monday was chess club; Tuesday was tennis; Wednesday was debating society; Thursday was piano; and Friday was time spent with friends. The weekends were no less frantic: Thomas played football on Saturdays and spent Sundays online gaming.

Tommy hadn't made friends in the area, but he didn't like being in the flat, so he spent time at a local cafe because they had free Wi-Fi and didn't ask questions so long as it wasn't too busy, and he sat quietly in a corner. It was warm and bright. There was a plug to charge his phone, and the tap water was free. He couldn't use the local library because it got closed just like the community centre where he used to live. Until the community centre closed, he would often go to the youth club there on Thursdays to use the computers or play sports.

Thomas thought he got too much homework, but it wasn't too hard. His mum and dad helped him whenever needed – and there was always his private tutor. His mum worked from home so was always on hand when needed; his dad ran his own business, so he organised his diary so he could pick Thomas up from chess club and debating society and watch him play football at the weekends.

Tommy knew his dad was a good man, but he lost his job in construction during Covid and struggled with the lockdowns. He became less patient, more prone to outbursts. Tommy's mum worked at the local supermarket and cleaned at the hospital. She worked shifts which could be tough. Some days, Tommy had to get his sister up and ready for school and some days he had to pick her up after school and babysit her till mum got home. There was no washing machine in the flat and the local launderette was expensive, so their clothes – which were too small – had to survive several wears. Tommy struggled to concentrate at school and often felt tired, hungry, and distracted. He would get into trouble for not doing his homework or for daydreaming in class. He would get behind because he was often late.

Thomas had easy manners, was confident and articulate. In the days before his dad bought a villa in Spain, the family would travel Europe. His weekends growing up were always busy – his parents liked to go to the theatre and to visit art galleries and museums. Books also featured heavily in his early memories. His dad would read to him most nights. His favourite author was Roald Dahl. The house was always full of books.

Tommy used to be eligible for the Pupil Premium. His mum didn't know why that stopped, something to do with changes to her Universal Credit. All she knew was that they didn't suddenly get any wealthier!

Thomas intended to stay on at school to do his A Levels then take a year out, travelling. After that, he wanted to go to university to read economics like his dad. His dad could get him a job in the city. He knew what he needed to get in his GCSEs and what A Levels would be best for university applications. He knew all his extra-curricular activities would help when it came to his UCAS form, too, and his parents had said that they'd help him financially.

Tommy had been feeling increasingly anxious. Anxious about school, about homework, about getting into trouble; anxious about not sleeping, not eating; anxious about his appearance, his health, his sister, his mum, where they were going to live next, what was going to happen to his dad.

Thomas was a high-performing student, predicted a raft of grade 9s in his GCSEs; Tommy was not. Thomas and Tommy were students at the same school. Thomas and Tommy had the same IQ. And yet there was little doubt that Thomas would outperform Tommy at school, not because he was brighter or harder working, but because he started the race halfway round the track and had more expensive running shoes.

So, what happened next?

Life after GCSEs

It's been a year since I last visited Thomas and Tommy. In the interim, they finished their GCSEs and completed Year 11. Thomas is now in the school sixth form studying A Levels; Tommy has enrolled at the local further education college where he's resitting his English and maths GCSEs alongside a Level 2 qualification in computing.

I meet Tommy on campus one wet November lunchtime. The college canteen is bustling with activity. Tommy has a tray of chips. The smell of salt and vinegar seduces me, and I instinctively place a hand to my stomach when I hear it grumble.

Tommy tells me about college. It wasn't his first choice, he says, but he didn't get the GCSE results he needed to stay on in the school sixth form. Nevertheless, he's enjoying it so far. There's more freedom, he tells me; you're treated more like an adult here than at school. Besides, his teachers at school never liked him, and he had few friends to speak of. The course he's on is easy, he says. Too easy, if he's honest. He did Computer Science GCSE so a lot of what they're doing in college this year is a step backwards for him. He had applied for the Level 3 course, but he hadn't met the entry requirements because he had needed grade 4s or higher in both English and maths.

I ask him why he didn't get the grades he needed. He says he knew his stuff, but the exam questions made no sense, used stupid words. The English language paper had a question about skiing holidays or something posh like that. He hadn't understood half of it. He wouldn't know a crampon if it bit him. And he hadn't understood a lot of the words in the unseen text extract either, couldn't catch hold of its meaning. Plus, he was tired and struggled to concentrate for the full 90 minutes. Kept drifting off, daydreaming. He started thinking about his mum who'd just lost her job cleaning at the local hospital. He'd think about his dad, too, who'd got into a bit of bother with the police after a fight outside his local pub. And he suspected his sister was being bullied at school because she had become quiet and withdrawn.

The maths exam was no better. He can add up, he says, but the questions were just too wordy. Shouldn't they test your maths not your English?

I ask Tommy if he revised for his exams. He says he tried but finding the time and space to study was always hard. And he lacked the motivation, he adds, candidly. In the spring, he had managed to get a part-time job clearing tables at the Polish cafe near his mum's flat because he knew he needed to help pay the bills now it was just him, his sister, and their mum. And the flat is tiny; he doesn't even have his own bed, he tells me, let alone a quiet corner in which to sit and work.

And the closer the exams got, the more he had begun to stress about them. He started having palpitations, panic attacks. He hadn't told his mum, as she had enough on her plate. School didn't help much; he said there was a homework club he could attend, but it was after school, and he needed to collect his sister from school so couldn't stay late.

Anyway, Tommy says, I've heard they've got to fail a third of students every year, so I guess I was unlucky, and they choose me. I ask him what he means, and he tells me it was something he'd heard a teacher say at school, but he hadn't really understood.

I ask Tommy if he'd have stayed on at school given the choice. He says he wanted to do A Levels because that's what most jobs ask for these days, but he'd had enough of the place, to be honest. He hadn't ever felt like he'd belonged there; the school wasn't really for people like him. What does he mean by "people like him", I ask. Working class kids, he says. Poor kids. It's not only the exams that talk about stupid skiing holidays or use big words, Tommy adds, growing morose, or perhaps truculent. His teachers seemed to be talking a different language half the time. He was always being told off, too, – getting detentions for not doing his homework or for not concentrating in class. Teachers don't understand what it's like for kids like him, he says.

Primary school had been a bit better. He was doing ok there. But then he moved to 'big school' and it all went downhill from there. His teachers thought he was thick, put him in the bottom sets and gave him boring work to do. Why did he get the impression his teachers thought he was thick, I ask. Don't really know, he says; maybe because I'm not as clever with words as some of the posh kids from up the hill. He didn't have their confidence, couldn't speak as well as them, and didn't always know how to explain his thoughts. He hadn't read all the books they'd read or been to all the places they'd been. Didn't play rugby at the weekends so often got left out, made to feel different.

I ask Tommy how he knows he was in all the bottom sets. He laughs, not cruelly, just suggesting the answer is obvious. He says everyone knew. They didn't call it the bottom set, but you only had to look around you to see that's what it was. All the estate kids, the ones from the children's home, the ones with no families, no money, no hope. All thrown in together. Sink or . . . well, sink. Besides, we were the ones who got the supply teachers all the time whilst the good teachers taught the clever kids, he says. We got wordsearches to do whilst they went on field trips or made things explode in the science labs. Not that we could have done the science experiments anyway – there were too many of us in our class, no room to swing a cat let alone dissect a frog. The top sets had half the number of students in them.

But is college good, I ask. Yeah. It's better than school, he says. More freedom, like I say. Not that I know what to do with it half the time because I don't have anywhere I can go to study, and the internet doesn't work in our block. Plus, I don't always know where to start, I get a lot of work to do outside lessons but where to begin? And I can't sit in the cafe and use their Wi-Fi anymore because I work there now, so they said it's not right.

I have to sit English and maths again, too, and the lessons are so boring. We just do the same stuff all over again. And many of the other students in those classes can't even speak English. I'm not racist, he says quickly, defensively. I don't mean anything bad by that. It's just a fact that a lot of the other students in my class are refugees or whatever, just arrived in England and can't understand the language so the teacher has to speak slowly: Small words, big pauses. That makes it boring for me, the lessons just drag.

So, what next? Tommy looks at me, confused. Do you mean after dinner? No, I explain. I mean, what's your plan for the future? Where do you see yourself going, what do you want to do with your life? He stares down at his chips for what seems like a long time, then faces me and says: Survive, I guess; get by. Earn enough to help my mum and sister out. I want my sister to go to uni, she's definitely got the brains for it. So have you, I tell him. I've seen your IQ score, your CATS and SATs. You're a bright lad. Yeah, well, maybe, he says. I wasn't the right kind of bright for school, though, was I? Or else I wouldn't be sitting here now.

The right kind of bright

You've got to be the right kind of bright, Thomas tells me as we sit at his kitchen island dipping bread sticks into a pot of organic hummus.

The right kind of bright? I ask. What does that mean? I'm good at exams, he says. It's not always what you know that matters – or how clever you are, your IQ or whatever. It's how good you are at remembering stuff and being able to write it all down in the time given and under pressure. Exams don't bother me, don't stress me out like they do some people. And I can write quickly, which helps. Good under pressure, me.

And you had lots of help at home, I suggest. Yes, I suppose so. My mum and dad are always around if I need help with homework or revision or whatever. Mum works from home and dad's his own boss so is there whenever I need him. And you had a private tutor, I add. Yes. Yes. I'm good at maths, Thomas says; get it from my dad. But the tutor helped me with my English because I was predicted a grade 7 and my parents wanted me to get straight grade 9s.

I'm good at remembering stuff, he repeats. Books I've read, places I've visited, things I've seen and heard. There was a question in the English exam about skiing and I remembered when me, mum, and dad went to Innsbruck – that's in Austria – on a skiing holiday. So, I used that memory, basically. The words just flowed.

It's not all about exams, though, is it, I ask. No, but the same applies in lessons, doesn't it? I mean, some people are more confident and able to explain themselves, others less so. I get my confidence from my dad. He says we belong wherever we are, should never feel excluded or isolated. We should be proud and speak our minds. Fit in everywhere. I know how to talk to teachers and people at my dad's work. Some kids just talk the same way to teachers as they do their mates and so they come a cropper.

How's sixth form, I ask. Thomas shrugs his shoulders: So-so. Is he enjoying the subjects he's chosen, no regrets? Well, they're what I need to get into uni so enjoyment isn't important really. He likes the fact he has some free study time, he says. Some days he can start school later, some days he can leave early. Gives him more time on his games console – where he earns money via his YouTube channel – and more time to shadow his dad who's given him an informal internship at his trading firm in the city. And he likes being independent, managing his own time and studies. His tutor helped him write a study plan and taught him something called the Pomodoro Technique. And he's been able to continue playing tennis and rugby.

Thomas tells me his plans for when he finishes sixth form have changed since we last met. He had intended to do Route 66, travelling across America in his gap year before university. But now he's decided to work full-time with his dad for a year because he knows this will increase his chances of getting into Cambridge, which is where his dad went. He'll be able to save enough money so he can enjoy university, too – get good digs and be able to join lots of clubs and socialise.

The rigged race of life

Thomas and Tommy went to the same school, and there were no discernible differences in their levels of intelligence. Whether they were equally gifted or equally average is of little consequence. What's important to note is that they were equal. And yet their lives were far from equitable. Thomas outperformed Tommy at every turn, and there's little doubt that he will continue to do so for the rest of their lives. He has already achieved a better level of education from school. He will go on to get better outcomes at post-16 and he will progress to university and secure a well-paid job and enjoy a meaningful and fulfilling professional career. His health and general well-being will be better than Tommy's, too.

In short, Thomas is destined to live a long, happy, rewarding life.

Tommy is not.

Tommy will struggle to achieve any worthwhile qualifications. He will struggle to find a good, well-paid job. He will struggle to afford a decent place to live. He will struggle to afford to heat his home or to feed himself healthily and adequately.

Tommy was born into a poor, working-class family which struggled to make ends meet and failed – not intentionally, but unavoidably and despite their best efforts – to provide a suitable start in life for Tommy and his sister. Unfortunately, Tommy's birth is set to be his destiny.

Had Thomas and Tommy been switched at birth, so too would their life chances be reversed. Despite what many privileged people may think, success is determined, not exclusively and not always, but in most cases, by the sheer luck of birth. It is much easier to be successful when you start the race halfway round the running track and have an expert coach and expensive equipment.

There are, of course, outliers, people who came from nothing but achieved much. But rags-to-riches stories like these are so rare as to be exceptions that prove the rule. And often these outliers, when you delve a little deeper, did benefit from circumstance. I consider myself to be such an example. I was born and brought up in a poor, working-class family and had no silver spoon. But I went on to be (relatively) successful in my field. I am now demonstrably middle-class: A professional with a raft of good qualifications, a homeowner, car owner, and taker of foreign holidays, able to fit in and feel comfortable in any social circle. But my journey was not one of individual means. Yes, I worked hard, I 'grafted' as we're told we must if we want to escape our disadvantage. But I was also lucky. I had good teachers and available and supportive parents who valued education and made sacrifices to ensure both my brother and I received a good education. I had free access to excellent public facilities including libraries and leisure centres. I was given a full government grant that enabled me to go to university. And often I was simply in the right place at the right time.

The fact remains that most people born into disadvantage or who have additional and different needs can not and do not escape that disadvantage, not because they are not bright enough or do not work hard enough, but because we do not live in a meritocracy and life is neither fair nor equitable.

But it doesn't have to be this way. Whilst society needs to change for there to be any meaningful and longstanding improvements to this situation, there are many changes that schools can make to help improve the educational and life chances of disadvantaged and vulnerable children, and to create a fairer, more equitable place to learn and thrive.

A call to action

Let us examine Tommy's experience of school and consider what his teachers could have done differently to help him achieve better outcomes and improve his life chances. In short, what could his teachers have done to prevent Tommy's birth from becoming his likely destiny?

Firstly, let's consider the importance of early intervention. Those children who start school at a disadvantage not only fail to catch up with their peers but find the attainment gap between them grows wider as they progress through the education system. The gap in vocabulary development between children in the top and bottom 20%

of incomes is, on average, 10 months at age 3 and 15 months by age 5. Forty-four percent of disadvantaged children meet the expected standards at age 11 (compared to 66% of non-disadvantaged children), but by the age of 16 only 25% of disadvantaged children achieve a grade 5 in English and maths GCSE (compared to 52% of non-disadvantaged children).

It follows, therefore, that the earlier we can intervene and address the differences between disadvantaged and non-disadvantaged learners, the greater the chance we will have of closing the gap. Tommy felt he was doing relatively well at primary school but struggled more and more as he got older and the gaps in his prior knowledge – or cultural capital – became bigger and more detrimental to his ability to access the school curriculum. Early intervention could have helped prevent Tommy's academic decline.

Secondly, there's the matter of transition. Another likely reason Tommy struggled as he got older is because he did not cope with the transfer from primary to secondary school very well. There could be several factors at play here. Tommy is less resilient than Thomas and hasn't been afforded the same opportunities to develop key character traits such as self-esteem. He also has difficulty remaining confident and comfortable in new, unfamiliar situations. Moving from a small primary school – the big fish in the small pond – where you're likely to be in the same classroom with the same teacher all day, to a large secondary school – the small fish in a large ocean – where you must quickly navigate changes of rooms and teachers, each with different routines and expectations, as well as the more complex social and emotional environment, is therefore challenging. Data transfer is also a factor. If Tommy's new teachers knew very little about him and his abilities beyond his SATs results, they may not have appreciated his true starting points and his learning preferences. If he was also struggling to adjust to the new environment, he may not have performed to the best of his abilities immediately upon changing schools and this may have been interpreted – wrongly – as a sign of low intelligence.

Had his new teachers been provided with more information about Tommy, such as what he was capable of producing outside of test conditions and beyond the core subjects, what motivates and demotivates him, how he likes to learn and demonstrate his learning, what gaps might exist in his knowledge and skills and life experiences, and perhaps even some information about his life outside of school, then they may have been better placed to assess his starting points and provide the support he needed.

Thirdly, we must consider the possibility that Tommy's teachers had biases or set expectations of what he could achieve based on his disadvantaged status and the way he presented himself in class – both physically and intellectually. They may have had pre-conceived notions of what someone like Tommy could achieve and, albeit with the best of intentions, they may have lowered their expectations, assuming Tommy was less able.

Certainly, it has been common practice in many schools and for many years to 'support' learners like Tommy through differentiation whereby those with differences and disadvantages are given a reduced or 'dumbed down' curriculum offer and easier tasks to do in class. Likewise, feedback has tended to be less demanding and expectations lower. As I say, this is often with good intentions, perhaps assuming learners like Tommy can't access a more ambitious curriculum and would simply flounder, and perhaps assuming easier work and less challenging feedback would inspire success and that this would motivate them to do better. But it doesn't often work that way. If we place a glass ceiling on what disadvantaged learners can achieve and then expect less of them, they will perform less well and we will simply double-down on their existing differences and disadvantages, rather than use education as a means of driving social justice and levelling the playing field.

We need to accept that it's not about ability. A disadvantaged learner is not necessarily less able than a non-disadvantaged learner, just as a learner with SEND is not necessarily less able than a non-SEND learner. We must not project biases and lower our expectations of these learners. Rather, we must have the same high expectations of all learners because the higher our expectations are, the better a learner will perform and the higher their expectations of themselves and their own abilities will be.

Fourthly, there's the fact that Tommy didn't feel like he belonged in school because he didn't see people like him teaching or leading the school, and what was taught and how it was taught didn't talk to him and his lived experiences.

Representation matters. If we do not see people like us or recognise the lives being presented to us as exemplars and heroes then we can assume we don't matter, we don't fit in, we don't belong here. Tommy did not see people like him at the front of class, nor did the curriculum content choices being made by his teachers truly reflect his life and community. The analogies used by his teachers to compare new, abstract ideas to something supposedly familiar and concrete failed to 'land' because he did not have the necessary frame of reference or the same 'cultural capital' as his more affluent and advantaged peers. And the examples used in assessments were similarly alien to him. Likewise, a lot of the language used by his teachers in class and in assessments was unfamiliar to him because he had gaps in his vocabulary.

Fifthly, Tommy was put into 'bottom sets' in some subjects because his school decided to set learners according to their ability. Sometimes this is unavoidable because of the constraints of the external assessment system. For example, in maths there are tiered exam papers at GCSE and students need to be taught the appropriate content to be prepared for either the higher or foundation tier. But in most subjects, this is not the case, and evidence suggests setting by ability is ineffective, or at least unproven practice. It certainly seems not to work well for those placed in lower ability classes who often become demotivated and who do not have ready access to higher-performing peers who provide aspirational role models and examples of higher attainment.

What's more, in Tommy's case, as is also common, the lower sets were taught by less experienced teachers and, worse, by transient teachers who did not know the learners very well. This is no criticism of supply teachers who work hard and have difficult jobs. But Tommy needs teachers who know him well. Often, the most experienced and proven teachers – such as the head of department – teach the top sets when it is the lower sets (populated by those most in need of expert, aspirational teachers and by those who experience the greatest challenges at school) which should be prioritised when it comes to timetabling.

It's also the case that in Tommy's 'bottom set' classes the teachers appeared to 'dumb down' curriculum content and make use of the traditional forms of differentiation I mentioned earlier. What Tommy needed was access to the same ambitious curriculum as his peers and teachers with high expectations of his abilities and capabilities.

Not all learners are equal. Some have more significant gaps in their prior knowledge and skills, including in their vocabulary and language and literacy skills, but the answer is not to do less for these learners; rather, it is to do more. We should give all learners access to the same ambitious, broad and balanced, and planned and sequenced curriculum – to the same models of excellence in each subject discipline – and then we should make that curriculum accessible to all learners by doing more or different things for those who start with less – including in the form of task-scaffolding.

Sixthly, Tommy lacked confidence in class and was reluctant to contribute to classroom discussions or even to articulate his thinking and demonstrate his learning. As well as issues of self-esteem, Tommy struggled with his oracy skills – he did not know how to express his thoughts or engage in debates and discussions. His more advantaged peers, like Thomas, not only had access to debating societies and other enrichment activities that helped build confidence and articulacy, but they also grew up in language-rich environments and were taught to express themselves with confidence and certainty. They learnt the art of code-switching, too, so that they could adapt to different situations and fit in, using the most appropriate vocabulary and register.

In addition, learners like Thomas grew up surrounded by books and other reading materials and thus developed a penchant for reading for pleasure and, with it, a wider knowledge of the world and a bigger vocabulary. Their frame of reference is therefore larger and thus they understand more of what is taught in school and how it is taught, including the analogies teachers use. The more you know, the easier it is to know more, and so Thomas makes good progress through school whilst Tommy does not.

Next, the system of assessment and the qualification framework further disadvantages learners like Tommy. Tommy is less able to prepare for exams and other high-stakes assessments because he does not have a home-life conducive to independent study nor the resources to study at home, including physical resources such as access to an internet-enabled device and books and stationery, and human resources such as a parent or other adult who is present and able to help. Tommy also struggles to find the time and space to engage in independent study and lacks motivation because he is often tired and hungry and stressed.

Furthermore, Tommy has not been taught how to organise his time nor how to maintain his concentration and motivation. He has not been helped to develop coping strategies to help manage his anxiety about exams and how to respond when presented with unfamiliar words or ideas in an exam.

We've already explored the vocabulary gap and know that Tommy has difficulty understanding some of the language used in class. But this is also a barrier in exams where the language demand has increased in recent years, including in subjects such as maths and science. A lack of cultural capital will also pose a problem in exams – such as having no first-hand experience of skiing or indeed of any foreign travel.

Life is not fair and neither is school. The disadvantaged and vulnerable are further disadvantaged by an education system that privileges the privileged.

But, as I say, it doesn't have to be this way. So, let's explore some practical ways in which we can change the system, include the excluded, and foster inclusion and belonging in the classroom . . .

2 Equality, diversity, and inclusion

Figure 2.1 EDI is about fairness

Taken together, equality, diversity, and inclusion (EDI) provide the foundations of a fair and thriving environment.

In schools, these principles ensure that all learners – regardless of their backgrounds, starting points, and additional and different needs – have equitable access to a high-quality education which will open doors to their future success. In schools, equality, diversity, and inclusion ensure that all learners feel valued as part of the community.

In short, equality, diversity, and inclusion are about belonging, being a full and active member of the community in which you live and learn and being given a fair chance of success at school and in life.

Equality, diversity, and inclusion – especially when used in the initialism form of EDI – are often assumed to be synonymous, forging one principle, but the distinct meanings of each of those three words are of importance and well worthy of dissection . . .

E is for equality – this means ensuring everyone has the same opportunities, removing barriers that prevent individuals from achieving their potential. Crucially, this does not mean treating everyone identically but rather equitably, accounting for different needs.

D is for diversity – this means celebrating the differences between people, recognising and valuing the varied backgrounds, identities, and perspectives that enrich a learning community.

I is for inclusion – this goes a step further, ensuring that diverse individuals feel welcomed, valued, and respected, and are able to participate fully in school life and are helped to prepare for full and active participation in wider society, both now and as adults.

To embed these three principles in our schools, we must first understand why some learners sometimes feel excluded. Feeling excluded, different, or *other*-ed stems from a combination of factors, including though not limited to:

Systemic barriers

- *Policies*: Policies or practices that assume a 'one-size-fits-all' approach can disadvantage those with specific needs, such as learners with learning difficulties or disabilities, or those with additional responsibilities at home such as caregiving.
- *Resources*: Learning materials that lack representation of diverse voices can alienate learners who do not see themselves reflected in what we teach and how we teach it.

Social barriers

- *Under-representation*: Learners from underrepresented groups may struggle to find peers who share their experiences, leading to feelings of loneliness.
- *Micro-aggressions*: Subtle, often unintentional acts of bias can erode a sense of belonging.

Practical barriers

- *Poverty*: Financial hardship can exclude learners from extracurricular activities or limit their ability to focus on their studies.
- *Logistics*: Learners who travel to school from a distance, perhaps as a consequence of family relocation or being moved into emergency accommodation, may find it harder to engage with school life, missing out on informal networks of support.

Building a genuinely inclusive school environment in which all learners feel they belong requires strategic and deliberate action. Here are some initial suggestions of how we might begin to foster a better sense of equality, diversity, and inclusion:

1. Embed EDI in policy and practice

We could:

- Ensure that all policies, from admissions to assessment, prioritise equity and inclusivity
- Regularly review curricula to include diverse voices, perspectives, and case studies

For example, in English we might include works by authors from different cultural backgrounds to reflect the diversity of the learner body.

2. Empower staff and learners

We could:

- Train staff to recognise unconscious bias, challenge discrimination, and model inclusive behaviour
- Establish learner-led inclusion groups to amplify underrepresented voices and foster peer support

For example, we could host workshops where learners and staff collaborate to identify and address barriers to inclusion.

3. Celebrate diversity

We could:

- Organise events that highlight different cultures, identities, and perspectives
- Use visual displays and communications to celebrate the diversity of our school community

For example, we could create a calendar of cultural awareness days, ensuring all celebrations are equally valued and visible.

4. Prioritise well-being and accessibility

We could:

- Provide accessible facilities, learning materials, and technology to support all learners
- Offer well-being services, including mental health support, tailored to diverse needs

For example, we could introduce quiet study zones or sensory-friendly areas for neurodiverse learners.

***

Whatever strategies we deploy, to be a truly inclusive school, we must continually assess our practices, and we must involve staff, learners, parents and families, governors, and external stakeholders in the process. This can, in part, be achieved by auditing three sets of factors:

1. **School-based factors, such as:**

   - *Representation*: Do leadership teams, teaching staff, and guest speakers reflect the diversity of the learner body?
   - *Environment*: Are school spaces physically and socially inclusive, from accessible buildings to gender-neutral bathrooms?
   - *Engagement*: Are learner feedback mechanisms inclusive and responsive to diverse needs?

2. **Home-based factors, such as:**

   - *Parental involvement*: Are parents and families from all backgrounds actively engaged with the school?
   - *Digital access*: Do all learners have the technology and internet access needed to participate fully in learning?
   - *Support networks*: Are there systems in place to support learners with challenging home lives, such as young carers or those in foster care?

3. **Learner-based factors, such as:**

   - *Belonging*: Do learners feel safe, respected, and valued within the school?
   - *Engagement*: Are learners from all backgrounds participating in extra-curricular activities, clubs, societies, and junior leadership opportunities such as the school council?
   - *Achievement*: Are there gaps in attainment between different groups of learners, and if so, what interventions are in place, and do they work?

Equality, diversity, and inclusion are about creating a school environment where every learner can thrive. By understanding barriers to belonging, fostering a culture of inclusion, and rigorously auditing our practices, we can better ensure that no learner is left behind and that education is used as a force for social justice and personal growth, empowering every individual to achieve their potential and contribute to a richer, more diverse society.

Self-evaluation

Having read about equality, diversity, and inclusion, put the theory into practice by answering the following self-evaluative questions:

1. How do I personally define equality, diversity, and inclusion, and how does this align with the definitions provided in this chapter?
2. Which barriers to EDI mentioned in the text are most relevant to my school? How can I address them effectively?
3. Are the policies I am responsible for or contribute to genuinely inclusive, or do they reflect a 'one-size-fits-all' approach?
4. Does the curriculum I teach, or support, include diverse voices and perspectives? If not, what specific changes can I advocate for or implement?
5. Have I taken steps to identify and address any unconscious biases I might hold?
6. How inclusive is my approach to engaging learners, staff, or colleagues from underrepresented groups?
7. How do I currently empower others (staff, learners, peers) to voice their perspectives and feel included in decision-making processes?
8. How well does my school celebrate diversity? Can I think of new initiatives or events that would enhance this celebration?
9. How often do I audit or review practices for inclusivity, and do I involve diverse stakeholders in this process?
10. After reading this chapter, what is one actionable step I can take immediately to promote equality, diversity, and inclusion in my work?

3 The 3Cs of inclusion

My 3Cs of inclusion are:

1. Culture

2. Collaboration

3. Curriculum

Culture

In an inclusive culture, every member of the school community is made to feel welcome and treats one another with dignity and respect. Learners help each other, and staff collaborate with each other. School staff and parents and families work as partners to support learners. The local community is fully involved in school life, and leaders and governors work productively together for the benefit of the school.

In an inclusive culture, there are high expectations for all learners, no matter their backgrounds, starting points, and additional needs, and all learners are equally valued. Staff seek to remove barriers to learning and participation in all aspects of the school, and everyone strives to minimise discriminatory practices.

Collaboration

Inclusive schools believe in collaboration over competition, they foster a sense of community, or team spirit, and of shared endeavour – working together towards a common goal, sharing success and failure.

In collaborative schools, staff appointments and promotions are fair, and all new staff are helped to settle into the school. These schools seek to admit all learners from their locality and make their buildings physically accessible to all people. All new learners are helped to settle into the school, and teaching groups are organised so that all learners are valued.

All forms of support are coordinated, and staff development activities help staff to respond to learner diversity. The Special Educational Needs Code of Practice is used to reduce the barriers to learning and participation of all learners. Support for those learning English as an additional language is coordinated with learning support. Pastoral and behaviour support policies are linked to curriculum development and learning support policies, and barriers to attendance are reduced.

Curriculum

In inclusive schools, teaching is planned with the learning of all learners in mind. Lessons encourage the participation of all learners. Learners are actively involved in their own learning, and they learn collaboratively. Assessment contributes to the achievements of all learners. Classroom discipline is based on mutual respect.

Teachers plan, teach, and assess in partnership. Teaching assistants support the learning and participation of all learners. Homework contributes to the learning of all, and all learners take part in activities outside the classroom.

Taken together, the 3Cs are about:

- Treating all learners and staff with equal value and respect
- Promoting greater learner participation while reducing exclusion from school cultures, communities, and curricula
- Adapting school cultures, policies, and practices to meet the diverse needs of all learners
- Removing barriers to learning and participation for every learner, not just those with disabilities or identified special educational needs
- Using lessons learned from addressing individual challenges to improve access and participation for all learners
- Seeing learner differences as assets for learning, rather than problems to solve
- Respecting every learner's right to receive an education in their local community
- Enhancing school environments for both staff and learners
- Highlighting the role of schools in fostering community, values, and relationships alongside academic achievement
- Building strong, supportive relationships between schools and their communities
- Understanding that inclusion in education contributes to broader social inclusion

What does this look like in the classroom?

To make inclusion tangible in the classroom, I'd suggest we focus on three areas of professional practice:

1. Planning

2. Teaching

3. Assessment

Let's start with planning . . .

Inclusive planning

An inclusive curriculum is one that reflects, celebrates, and supports the diverse experiences of all learners. It acknowledges the richness of the communities we serve while equipping learners with the knowledge and skills they need to thrive in an interconnected world. Achieving this requires a deliberate approach to curriculum design, ensuring that every learner feels seen, valued, and empowered.

The key to designing an inclusive curriculum forms my 3Rs:

1. Reflect

2. Reveal

3. Review

Reflect

An inclusive curriculum should act as a mirror, reflecting the lived experiences of learners and helping them connect their learning to their own personal and cultural identities. When learners see themselves represented in what they study, this fosters a sense of belonging, raises aspirations, and improves engagement.

Here are some practical suggestions of how we might make the curriculum a mirror . . .

1. Incorporate local and cultural contexts by tailoring topics to include references to the local area, history, and culture, as well as the broader cultural heritage of our learner body. For example, in a geography lesson we might explore the environmental challenges or urban planning issues relevant to the community in which our school is based.

2. Include diverse role models by highlighting figures from a range of backgrounds in subject areas. For example, we might celebrate scientists, authors, and leaders who

represent a variety of ethnicities, genders, and abilities. In science, for instance, we might include profiles of notable scientists such as Dr Maggie Aderin-Pocock or Tu Youyou.

3. Draw on learners' experiences by inviting them to share their perspectives, stories, and cultural practices as part of their learning journey. For example, in a food technology class we might ask learners to share family recipes and explore the cultural significance of these dishes.

Reveal

As well as being a mirror, an inclusive curriculum should also act as a window, revealing a life, or lives, beyond learners' own lived experiences, exposing them to the diversity and richness of the wider world. This is an opportunity to challenge stereotypes, broaden horizons, and instil a sense of curiosity and empathy.

Here are some practical suggestions of how we might make the curriculum a window . . .

1. Expose learners to global perspectives by incorporating content that explores cultures, histories, and traditions from around the world, encouraging learners to understand and respect diversity. For example, in history we might balance the study of British history with topics such as the Silk Road, the Mali Empire, or the Indian independence movement.

2. Challenge prejudice and bias by using the curriculum to dismantle stereotypes and promote critical thinking about discrimination and inequality. For example, in English we might explore texts that examine social justice issues, such as *To Kill a Mockingbird* or *Noughts and Crosses*.

3. Celebrate multilingualism by valuing the linguistic diversity of learners by encouraging the exploration of multiple languages and dialects. For example, we might offer language electives that reflect the languages spoken in our community, such as Urdu, Polish, or Somali.

Review

To ensure the curriculum meets the needs of all learners, it must be regularly reviewed and adapted. An inclusive curriculum is not static; rather, it evolves alongside the community it serves. As such, we need to audit textbooks, images, and lesson materials to ensure they reflect a diverse range of people, cultures, and experiences. For example, we could check for gender balance and cultural diversity in illustrations and examples used in maths problems or science experiments.

We also need to ensure that the curriculum includes both traditional and non-traditional narratives, recognising the contributions of marginalised groups. In art, for instance, we might go beyond the European canon to include artists such as Yayoi Kusama or El Anatsui.

We could also use surveys, focus groups, and open forums to gather feedback on how well the curriculum meets the needs of learners and reflects their identities. For example, we could ask learners if they feel represented in their lessons and what additional topics they would like to explore. A further suggestion would be to work with colleagues to identify gaps and overlaps in curriculum coverage, ensuring a cohesive approach to inclusion. We might, for example, link English lessons on persuasive writing with geography discussions about climate change activism.

Making the curriculum more inclusive is not a one-off task but rather an ongoing commitment. By using the curriculum as both a mirror to reflect learners' lived experiences and a window to celebrate diversity, we can begin to create an educational environment where every learner feels valued and inspired.

Through regular auditing and collaboration, we can then ensure our curriculum evolves to meet the changing needs of our learners as well as those of the wider world. In doing so, we can empower learners to embrace their own identities, celebrate differences, and contribute positively to an inclusive and equitable society.

That's planning, but what of teaching? How can we make sure the way in which we translate our lesson plans into classroom practice is also inclusive of all our learners?

Inclusive teaching

Inclusive teaching is about ensuring that every learner, regardless of their background, ability, or starting point, can access and benefit from the same ambitious curriculum.

Inclusive teaching involves balancing high expectations of all with thoughtful support for those who need it when they need it, ensuring that all learners feel valued and empowered to succeed.

The key to inclusive teaching forms my 3Ds:

1. Diagnose

2. Deliver

3. Differentiate

Let's explore each in turn . . .

Diagnose

To teach inclusively, we must first understand the individual starting points and additional needs of our learners. This insight allows us to tailor our teaching and ensure every learner has a fair chance of success.

To achieve this, we might use diagnostic assessments and start by identifying what learners already know and what gaps need to be addressed. This could involve baseline tests, prior work reviews, or simple classroom discussions. For example, at the start of a new topic, we could ask learners to complete a quick quiz or mind map to assess prior knowledge. We might also work with support staff, parents, and learners themselves to understand any additional needs, such as SEND, language barriers, or socio-economic challenges. We could, for instance, use Individual Education Plans (IEPs) and learner profiles to inform lesson planning.

We also need to pay attention to how learners engage in lessons. Non-verbal cues, such as hesitation or frustration, can signal unmet needs. A learner who consistently avoids contributing to class discussions may benefit from sentence starters or smaller group work. As such, as well as conducting an initial and diagnostic assessment, we need to make use of ongoing low-stakes formative assessments to ensure we continue to meet the needs of all learners.

Deliver

Inclusive teaching doesn't mean diluting the curriculum. Instead, it's about providing the support necessary for all learners to engage with the same challenging and meaningful content.

This means we must set high expectations for everyone and believe that every learner is capable of achieving success and then communicate this belief consistently. We must, therefore, avoid simplifying language unnecessarily; instead, we need to explicitly teach key vocabulary to support understanding.

We also need to present material in varied formats – such as visual aids, diagrams, videos, or practical demonstrations – to support different approaches to learning. When introducing a new concept in science, for example, we could use models or experiments alongside written explanations.

We then need to prioritise the mastery of core concepts over covering large amounts of content superficially. For example, in maths we might spend extra time ensuring all learners understand fractions before moving on to percentages.

Differentiate

Inclusivity means being flexible and responsive in the moment, as well as planning ahead to meet diverse needs. As such, we should regularly check for understanding during lessons and adjust our teaching based on what learners demonstrate they know and can do. We might pose targeted questions or use mini whiteboards to assess understanding before moving on. We should also be prepared to adapt activities on the spot if learners are struggling. If a learner struggles with a group task, for example, we might provide a simplified version of the instructions or allocate specific roles. We need to anticipate barriers and plan scaffolded or differentiated resources in advance. In a history lesson, for example, we might prepare simplified timelines or glossaries for learners who may find the topic overwhelming.

Some learners require more support to bridge the gap between their starting point and the ambitious outcomes we expect. Task-scaffolding is a practical way to achieve this. This requires us to:

- Break down tasks into smaller steps and provide clear, manageable stages to help learners tackle complex tasks without feeling overwhelmed. When teaching essay writing, for example, we could start with a single paragraph structure before moving on to full essays.

- Model expectations and show learners what success looks like by modelling answers, problem-solving methods, or completed tasks. For example, we might solve a maths problem step-by-step on the board, narrating our thought process as we go.

- Use structured support such as sentence starters, writing frames, or checklists to help learners organise their work. In English, for example, we might offer a paragraph structure such as *Point, Evidence, Explanation* to guide learners' responses.

- Gradually remove support as learners grow in confidence and ability, reducing scaffolding to encourage independence. For example, we might start by providing a detailed writing frame, then gradually shift to an outline, and finally encourage learners to create their own structure.

Inclusive teaching is not about creating separate pathways for different learners but rather ensuring that all learners can access and thrive within the same ambitious curriculum. By diagnosing starting points, planning and teaching with flexibility, and scaffolding tasks appropriately, we can create an environment where every learner feels supported and challenged.

Ultimately, inclusivity is about believing in every learner's potential and doing whatever it takes to help them succeed.

That's teaching, now for assessment . . .

Inclusive assessment

Assessments – when done well – can provide crucial insights into what learners know and can do. However, to be truly effective, assessments must be inclusive – designed and delivered in such a way that allows all learners, regardless of their needs or circumstances, to demonstrate their learning and progress.

The key to making our assessments more inclusive forms my 3As:

1. Accessibility

2. Adjustments

3. Assistive technologies

Let's explore each in turn . . .

Accessibility

Inclusive assessments start with accessibility, ensuring that all learners can engage with the process itself. Barriers – whether physical, cognitive, or emotional – must be removed in order to provide every learner with a fair opportunity to succeed and demonstrate their success.

Here are some top tips for making assessment accessible:

1. Use plain language and avoid unnecessary jargon when explaining tasks. Consider visual aids or examples to supplement written instructions. For example, replace "Define and analyse the socio-political ramifications of the Industrial Revolution" with "Explain what the Industrial Revolution was and how it changed society".

2. Present information in a variety of ways – written, oral, visual – to accommodate different learning preferences and needs. For example, allow learners to access exam questions on paper, as audio files, or through braille as needed.

3. Ensure that time allocations reflect the complexity of the task, accounting for processing or mobility challenges some learners may face. For example, allow extra time for learners with dyslexia to complete reading-heavy assessments.

4. Minimise external stressors such as noise, distractions, or unclear rules, and provide a calm, structured setting. For example, arrange a quiet room with noise-cancelling headphones for learners sensitive to sensory overload.

Adjustments

Not all learners can show what they know through traditional assessment methods. Reasonable adjustments enable learners to demonstrate their learning without being unfairly hindered by barriers unrelated to the knowledge or skills being tested.

This might mean allowing learners to choose how they present their knowledge, whether through essays, presentations, diagrams, or practical demonstrations. For example, for a history assessment, a learner might choose to write an essay, record a spoken narrative, or create a timeline with annotations.

This might mean focusing on the specific knowledge or abilities being assessed, rather than unrelated elements such as handwriting or spelling. For example, in a science test on ecosystems, we might allow a learner to type or dictate their answers rather than writing by hand if motor skills are a barrier.

This might also mean, where appropriate, modifying success criteria to reflect individual needs while maintaining high expectations. For example, we might assess a learner's understanding of narrative structure in creative writing rather than penalising them for spelling errors due to dyslexia.

Assistive technologies

Assistive technologies can also play a powerful role in making assessments more inclusive, helping learners overcome barriers and focus on the knowledge or skills being evaluated. Software such as speech-to-text, spell checkers, and grammar tools can help learners with language processing challenges express their ideas more effectively. For example, we could allow learners to use dictation tools during essay-based assessments.

Digital assessments can be customised to suit individual needs, such as altering font sizes, colours, or line spacing. For example, we could use online platforms that allow learners to adjust text display or include screen readers for visually impaired learners.

We could also use tools such as calculators, concept-mapping software, or prompts to help learners focus on the key learning objectives. In a maths assessment, for instance, we could provide a learner with ADHD access to a digital tool that helps organise multi-step problem-solving tasks. Further, we could allow learners to use video or audio tools to create presentations or demonstrate learning in creative ways.

To repeat: Inclusive assessment is not about lowering expectations but about ensuring every learner has a fair chance to succeed and a fair chance to demonstrate their learning and progress. By making assessment methods accessible, offering reasonable adjustments, and embracing assistive technology, we can create an environment where all learners can show their true capabilities.

What's more, when assessments are inclusive, they become more accurate, providing a clearer picture of what learners know and can do. Most importantly, inclusive assessments send a powerful message: That every learner's potential matters, and that their success is worth the effort it takes to remove barriers and level the playing field.

We will explore inclusive lesson planning, teaching, and assessment in more detail later.

Self-evaluation

Having read about the 3Cs of inclusion, put the theory into practice by answering the following self-evaluative questions:

1. How effectively does my school create an inclusive culture where every member of the community feels valued and respected? What improvements could I make to strengthen this?

2. Do I foster a sense of teamwork and shared goals in my classroom or school? How can I better balance collaboration with competition?

3. How well does my curriculum reflect and celebrate the diversity of my learners? Are there gaps in representation that I need to address?

4. How often do I incorporate learners' personal and cultural experiences into lesson content? Could I do more to make learners feel represented?

5. How well does my curriculum expose learners to diverse perspectives and challenge stereotypes? What specific steps can I take to broaden horizons further?

6. Do I regularly review my curriculum to ensure it meets the evolving needs of all learners? How do I gather and act on feedback to enhance inclusivity?

7. Am I effectively identifying and responding to the diverse needs and starting points of my learners? Are my diagnostic tools and methods sufficient?

8. Do I set high expectations for all learners while providing the necessary support? How could I make my teaching more accessible and engaging?

9. How effectively do I scaffold tasks and adapt teaching strategies to meet the varied needs of my learners? What adjustments could I implement to ensure no learner feels excluded?

10. Are my assessment methods fair and accessible to all learners? Am I making the best use of reasonable adjustments and assistive technologies to help learners demonstrate their full potential?

PART TWO
Mind the gaps

In order to achieve inclusion and belonging, we first need to understand who is not yet included in school life and who does not yet feel as if they belong in our classroom.

To answer these questions, let's consider some of the causes of the most stubborn and longstanding attainment gaps . . . We'll examine the gender gap, the ethnicity gap, the SEND gap, the socio-economic gap, the vulnerable children gap, and the mobility gap, as well as some of the in-school factors that exclude some learners from full participation.

Let's start with the gender gap . . .

4 The gender gap

While the nature and scale of the gender gap vary by context, the general trend is that girls tend to outperform boys in GCSEs and A levels. This disparity is particularly stark in subjects like English, while boys may perform slightly better in some STEM subjects, though this varies.

In 2023, 30% of girls achieved grade 7/A or above at GCSE, compared to 22.6% of boys. This represents a gap of 7.4 percentage points. The pass rate (grade 4/C or above) was 74.4% for girls and 67.4% for boys, a gap of 7 percentage points. Girls outperform boys significantly in reading and writing. The 2022 SATs for Key Stage 2 revealed that 73% of girls met the expected standard in reading, writing, and maths, compared to 65% of boys. Boys are 3.7 times more likely than girls to have special educational needs related to literacy.

In 2023, 25.1% of girls achieved A* or A grades at A Level, compared to 21.5% of boys. Girls are more likely to take and excel in subjects like English, psychology, and biology, while boys dominate in physics, maths, and computer science.

Girls are more likely to progress to higher education, with 57% of female school leavers entering university in 2022 compared to 44% of male school leavers.

These gaps are stubborn and persistent, but there has been some movement over the last couple of decades. The gap in GCSE performance has remained relatively consistent since the early 2000s. However, the introduction of reformed GCSEs in 2017 – featuring more exam-based assessments – led to a slight narrowing of the gap, as boys tend to perform better in high-stakes exams than in coursework.

The gender gap in A Level results has been more volatile. Historically, girls have outperformed boys in A Levels overall, but boys tend to do better in maths and physics, fields that have grown in popularity recently.

Over the last 20 years, the gap in university participation has widened. In 2000, the difference in higher education entry rates between men and women was around 5 percentage points; by 2022, it had grown to over 13 percentage points.

The pandemic widened the gender attainment gap, particularly in GCSEs, as girls tended to adapt better to remote learning, demonstrating greater self-regulation and organisation.

Initiatives such as curriculum reform and a focus on STEM education for girls have addressed some disparities, but the persistent gap in literacy and overall attainment between boys and girls shows that more work is needed.

Several factors contribute to this phenomenon:

- Cultural expectations and stereotypes: Boys and girls are often subject to different societal or family pressures. For example, boys may feel discouraged from engaging in activities seen as traditionally feminine, such as reading for pleasure, which is crucial for literacy development. Conversely, girls are often socialised to adopt behaviours that align well with the structure of formal education, such as organisation and attention to detail. I say again that these are stereotypes or societal attitudes not the facts of the matter, and certainly not related to biological differences. There is no reason why reading for pleasure should be considered feminine nor any evidence that girls are innately more organised than boys.

- Engagement and motivation: Studies suggest that boys are less likely than girls to find classroom learning engaging. This may be due to teaching methods that favour quiet, collaborative work, which aligns better with the behaviours often encouraged in girls more than boys.

- Curriculum and assessment: The UK education system relies heavily on written, often essay-based, assessments, areas where girls traditionally excel. Boys, who may perform better in high-pressure, time-constrained tasks, could be disadvantaged by this emphasis.

- Role models: The shortage of male teachers in primary education means young boys might not see positive academic role models who reflect their own identity. This absence can reinforce the stereotype that learning isn't for them.

- Behaviour and discipline: Boys are more likely to be excluded from school and to have behavioural issues that interfere with learning. Disruption in the classroom can hinder their progress compared to their female peers.

Is the gender gap caused by nature or nurture?

In the blue corner: nature

There are some biological factors worth considering:

- Developmental differences: On average, boys' brains develop more slowly than girls', particularly in areas related to language and self-regulation. This can mean boys struggle with literacy and the organisational demands of schooling at an early age.

- Neurological variations: Research suggests that boys may be more prone to risk-taking behaviours and find it harder to sit still or focus for long periods, potentially affecting their classroom engagement. Girls, on the other hand, may find verbal reasoning tasks easier, which could explain their higher achievement in subjects like English.

While these natural differences might explain certain trends in early education, they don't account for the consistent and widening gap seen throughout schooling. If biology were the sole factor, we would expect similar outcomes across all contexts, yet educational attainment gaps vary significantly between cultures and over time.

In the red corner: nurture

Nurture – shaped by environment, culture, and socialisation – plays a far greater role in creating and sustaining the gender attainment gap. Key factors include:

- Cultural expectations: Boys are often socialised to value physical activity, competition, and independence, while girls are encouraged to focus on cooperation, communication, and meticulousness. These traits align differently with traditional teaching styles, which reward sustained focus and organisational skills – traits girls are more likely to have been encouraged to develop.
- School environment: The structure of the education system often favours traits traditionally associated with girls. Essay-based assessments, for instance, reward detailed planning and reflection. Boys might excel in high-stakes exams but struggle with the ongoing demands of coursework.
- Role models and representation: Boys see fewer male role models in education, especially in primary schools. This can reinforce the idea that learning isn't a 'male' activity, leading to disengagement.
- Stereotypes and bias: Gendered assumptions can shape teacher expectations. For example, boys may be labelled as disruptive or 'less academic', which can affect their confidence and create a self-fulfilling prophecy.
- Engagement with reading: Girls are more likely to engage with reading for pleasure, which boosts literacy skills – a key foundation for success across the curriculum. Boys, by contrast, often view reading as 'uncool' or irrelevant, reflecting broader societal attitudes rather than innate preferences.

A split draw?

While it's important to acknowledge natural differences in approaches to learning, the solutions lie primarily in addressing the environmental and cultural factors that shape boys' educational experiences.

The gender attainment gap is not a product of biology alone. It is largely the result of societal influences and the ways in which schools interact with these. Addressing the gap is about creating an education system that works for everyone, acknowledging natural differences while focusing on nurturing each learner's potential. By doing so, we can ensure all children – regardless of gender – have the opportunity to thrive.

Addressing the gender attainment gap requires a multi-faceted approach:

Firstly, we could diversify teaching methods and adopt a range of pedagogical styles that appeal to different learning preferences. For instance, incorporating more hands-on, practical activities and competitive elements can help engage boys.

Secondly, we could promote literacy for boys and encourage reading through the use of topics and materials that interest boys. We can partner with libraries and parents to create initiatives like book clubs that feature action, adventure, and nonfiction texts.

Thirdly, we could challenge gender stereotypes and actively work to break down ingrained perceptions that discourage boys from engaging in academic pursuits. Initiatives such as highlighting successful male authors or female scientists can help change perceptions.

Fourthly, we could ensure there are more male role models in education. Recruiting more male teachers and mentors could have a positive impact, particularly in early years and primary settings. Role models help boys see that learning is valuable and achievable for them too.

Fifthly, we could provide behaviour support programmes, tailored interventions designed to help reduce classroom disruption and exclusion rates among boys. Early identification of those at risk and providing targeted support can keep boys engaged with their education.

Finally, we could rethink assessments and ensure a greater balance is struck between classwork – in its many forms – and exams which could help level the playing field. A more diversified approach to assessment would cater to different strengths across genders.

A call to action

In short, the gender attainment gap is not inevitable. By understanding its root causes and addressing them through thoughtful, evidence-based strategies, we can ensure that all learners, regardless of gender, have an equal opportunity to thrive. And this is not about disadvantaging girls, who have worked hard to close historical gaps in their own attainment. Rather, it's about recognising that boys and girls have different challenges and ensuring that no one is left behind.

How the gender gap intersects with inclusion and belonging

A sense of inclusion and belonging is fundamental to academic success. When learners feel valued, respected, and recognised in their learning environment, they are more likely to engage with their studies and achieve their potential. The gender attainment gap is closely tied to issues of inclusion and belonging, because boys and girls often experience schooling in ways that shape their confidence, motivation, and identity as learners.

Here are some ways in which the gender gap intersects with inclusion and belonging . . .

- Stereotypes and expectations: Boys may feel excluded from the classroom culture if they perceive learning as 'not for them'. This is often reinforced by stereotypes that boys should be boisterous or less academic, which can alienate those who don't conform. While girls generally perform better academically, they may feel excluded in certain subjects like STEM, where male dominance in representation and stereotypes can make them feel out of place.

- Role models: The lack of male teachers, particularly in primary schools, can make boys feel that education is a female-dominated sphere. Without relatable role models, boys might struggle to see learning as part of their identity. Conversely, girls in STEM subjects often lack female role models, which can lead to feelings of exclusion and discourage participation.

- Curriculum design: If the curriculum prioritises topics or methods of teaching that resonate more with one gender, the other may feel marginalised. For example, boys may feel less included when literacy is taught using materials that don't align with their interests, while girls may feel excluded from practical, hands-on activities that dominate some science lessons.

- Classroom culture: Schools that reward traits like compliance, meticulousness, and quietness may inadvertently favour girls, who are more likely to exhibit these behaviours due to societal expectations. Boys, who may prefer active or competitive environments, can feel excluded from this model of success.

- Peer dynamics: Boys often face pressure to adopt anti-academic attitudes to fit in with their peers. If trying hard at school is seen as 'uncool', boys may disengage to maintain social status. Similarly, girls in male-dominated fields like physics might feel outnumbered and isolated, deterring their participation.

How else can we narrow the gender gap?

In addition to what I suggested already, we might be well-advised to:

1. Foster a welcoming environment. We should cultivate a culture where all learners feel they belong. This involves challenging gender stereotypes and ensuring that classroom activities and interactions celebrate diversity in interests and strengths.

2. Expand role models: We should try to recruit more male teachers, especially in primary schools, to show boys that learning is not gendered. Where this is not

possible, we could look to male volunteers and mentors. We should also try to promote female success stories in STEM to inspire girls and create a sense of belonging in these fields.

3. Curriculum adaptation: We should endeavour to use texts, themes, and activities that reflect the interests and experiences of all learners. For boys, this might mean incorporating more action-based or non-fiction texts in literacy; for girls, showcasing collaborative and creative aspects of STEM.

4. Tailored teaching strategies: We might consider introducing a mix of teaching styles, such as active learning, group work, and independent study, to cater to different preferences. We might also encourage boys to see value in traditionally feminine traits, such as collaboration and organisation, while also celebrating girls' confidence in male-dominated subjects.

5. Mentorship and peer support: We might establish mentoring programmes where older learners can act as role models, breaking down gendered perceptions and encouraging belonging.

6. Staff training: We should endeavour to ensure that all school staff are trained to recognise how unconscious biases and classroom practices might inadvertently exclude boys or girls. Creating inclusive spaces where every learner feels respected is key.

Inclusion and belonging are not just about making learners feel comfortable – they are directly linked to achievement. The gender attainment gap often reflects how well boys and girls feel they belong in their learning environments. By fostering inclusion through thoughtful policies, teaching practices, and cultural shifts, we can help all learners succeed *and* close the gender gap.

Self-evaluation

Having read about the gender gap, put the theory into practice by answering the following self-evaluative questions:

1. Can you summarise the primary factors contributing to the gender attainment gap?

2. How does this chapter differentiate between biological and social factors affecting the gender gap? Do you agree with the emphasis placed on nurture over nature?

3. What insights did you gain about how current assessment methods impact boys' and girls' performance differently?

4. How do cultural expectations and stereotypes influence the gender attainment gap? Can you identify examples from your own experience?

5. Which of the proposed solutions for addressing the gender gap resonates most with you? Why?

6. How does the sense of inclusion and belonging intersect with academic achievement for boys and girls?

7. What steps could you take in your own educational or professional environment to reduce the gender attainment gap?

8. Why are role models important in education? How might their presence (or absence) impact boys and girls differently?

9. Reflect on how the curriculum in your context could be adapted to better cater to diverse learning styles across genders.

10. What, if any, limitations or biases did you notice in this chapter's arguments or proposed solutions? How might these affect the effectiveness of its suggestions?

5 The ethnicity gap

Moving on from gender, another major cause of attainment gaps is ethnicity. While some ethnic groups perform above the national average, others consistently achieve lower grades. Addressing this gap is crucial for creating a fair and equitable education system.

Data from GCSE results and other key measures highlight disparities among ethnic groups. For example:

- Learners from Chinese and Indian backgrounds tend to perform well above the national average at all levels of education.
- Learners from Black Caribbean, Pakistani, Bangladeshi, and Gypsy, Roma, and Traveller backgrounds often have lower attainment.
- Black African learners and those from Other White backgrounds (such as Eastern European migrants) show mixed results, often influenced by socio-economic factors and levels of English proficiency.

Here's a deeper dive into the data . . .

At GCSE (2022)

- Chinese learners: 81.1% achieved grade 5 or above in GCSE English and maths.
- Indian learners: 71.7% achieved grade 5 or above.
- White British learners: 52.7% achieved grade 5 or above.
- Black Caribbean learners: 33.3% achieved grade 5 or above.
- Gypsy/Roma learners: 6.2% achieved grade 5 or above.

At Key Stage 2 SATs (2022)

- In reading, writing, and maths combined, 80% of Chinese learners and 74% of Indian learners met the expected standard, compared to 65% of White British learners and 48% of Black Caribbean learners.

University progression (2021)

- Asian learners had the highest university entry rate at 72.7%, followed by Black learners at 59.7%.

- White learners had the lowest entry rate at 42.1%, though socio-economic background significantly affects these figures.

The ethnicity attainment gap has shifted significantly over the past two decades, with some groups improving dramatically while others continue to face challenges.

Learners from Bangladeshi and Pakistani backgrounds have seen substantial improvements in attainment. For example, in the early 2000s, Bangladeshi learners were among the lowest achievers, but now their performance is close to or above the national average. This progress is attributed to targeted interventions, increased parental engagement, and higher aspirations within these communities.

Black Caribbean learners, meanwhile, have consistently underperformed compared to other groups, with only marginal improvements over the years. Gypsy, Roma, and Traveller learners remain the lowest-performing group, with little change over two decades, reflecting deep-seated barriers including discrimination, high mobility, and poor attendance.

While socio-economic disadvantage affects all groups, its impact varies. For example, White learners eligible for free school meals (FSM) perform worse on average than FSM-eligible learners from most ethnic minority groups. This has shifted the focus from ethnicity alone to the intersection of ethnicity and poverty when tackling the attainment gap.

Changes to the curriculum and assessment methods, such as the removal of coursework from GCSEs, have affected different groups in varying ways. Learners from some ethnic minority backgrounds have adapted better to these changes due to stronger family support or community-driven aspirations. The pandemic widened gaps for some groups, particularly Black Caribbean and Gypsy/Roma learners, who were disproportionately affected by school closures and unequal access to online learning. Conversely, high-achieving groups like Chinese and Indian learners were less affected due to stronger access to resources at home.

The fact that some ethnicity gaps have narrowed but others remain stubbornly persistent suggests that progress is possible but not inevitable. Tackling the gap requires a continued focus on poverty and intersectional factors, recognising that socio-economic disadvantage exacerbates ethnic disparities. It requires a challenge to the systemic biases that lead to lower expectations for certain groups. And it requires tailored interventions to address the specific barriers faced by underperforming groups, such as improved attendance support for Gypsy/Roma learners and mentoring for Black Caribbean learners.

In terms of intersectional factors, we need to acknowledge that the ethnicity gap is the result of complex, overlapping factors which include:

- Socio-economic disadvantage: Learners from ethnic minority groups are more likely to experience poverty, which can limit access to resources like private tuition, technology, or quiet spaces for study. Schools in disadvantaged areas often have fewer resources and higher teacher turnover, affecting the quality of education.
- Language barriers: Learners from families where English is not the first language may face challenges in literacy-based subjects, particularly in their early years of education.
- Systemic bias and low expectations: Stereotypes and unconscious bias can result in teachers holding lower expectations for learners from certain ethnic backgrounds. This can affect how they are taught, disciplined, and assessed. Exclusion rates are higher for Black Caribbean learners, with many excluded for behaviour rather than supported with early interventions.
- Lack of representation: A lack of diverse role models in the curriculum and teaching workforce can make it harder for learners from minority backgrounds to feel a sense of belonging and aspiration. For example, a curriculum that centres on Western perspectives may fail to engage learners from non-Western backgrounds.
- Parental engagement: Cultural and linguistic differences can affect how families engage with the education system. Some parents may feel unable to navigate it effectively, particularly if they face language barriers or are unfamiliar with the structure.
- Peer dynamics: Learners from minority groups may face bullying or discrimination, leading to disengagement and lower self-esteem, which directly impact academic performance.

Because of this complexity, attempts to close the ethnicity gap will require system-wide efforts, addressing the root causes and tailoring interventions to meet the needs of different groups. These efforts might include:

1. Targeted support for disadvantaged learners: We need to use the Pupil Premium effectively to provide additional resources, such as one-to-one tuition, mentoring, and access to extracurricular activities. Early intervention programmes, particularly in literacy and numeracy, can also help learners from non-English-speaking backgrounds.

2. Anti-bias training for teachers: Regular training on unconscious bias can help teachers to set high expectations for all learners and to use fair and equitable classroom practices. We should also monitor exclusion rates and ensure behaviour policies are applied consistently across all groups.

3. Culturally inclusive curriculum: We need to diversify the curriculum to reflect the contributions and histories of all ethnic groups. This not only boosts engagement but also helps foster a sense of belonging. We might also encourage open discussions about race and identity to create a more inclusive school culture.

4. Improving representation in the workforce: We should make efforts to recruit and retain more teachers from ethnic minority backgrounds to provide diverse role models. We also need to support aspiring leaders from underrepresented groups to move into senior positions within schools.

5. Parental engagement programmes: We need to work with families to build stronger home-school links. This might include offering workshops for parents on how to support their children's learning or providing interpreters for non-English-speaking families. We can also work with community leaders to build trust and encourage greater participation.

6. Challenging stereotypes: We should actively challenge negative stereotypes through assemblies, workshops, and lessons. We can celebrate diversity by marking events like Black History Month or International Mother Language Day.

7. Mentorship and peer support: We should endeavour to establish mentoring schemes to connect learners with older learners or professionals from similar backgrounds who can offer guidance and encouragement. Peer support programmes can also help build confidence and foster positive relationships.

How the ethnicity gap intersects with inclusion and belonging

As we've already seen, a sense of inclusion and belonging is fundamental to academic success because when learners feel valued, respected, and recognised in their learning environment, they are more likely to engage, achieve, and thrive. The ethnicity gap is closely tied to whether learners from diverse backgrounds feel included in the school culture, community, and curriculum. Addressing this issue is key to narrowing the ethnicity gap and ensuring all learners reach their potential.

Here are some tangible ways in which the ethnicity gap intersects with inclusion and belonging . . .

- Curriculum representation: When the curriculum predominantly reflects Western perspectives, learners from minority ethnic backgrounds may feel excluded. For example, the lack of Black or Asian voices in history or literature can send the unspoken message that their contributions are less valued. This sense of exclusion can dampen engagement and reduce motivation, leading to lower attainment.

- Teacher expectations and bias: Stereotypes and unconscious bias can influence how teachers perceive and interact with learners. Studies show that Black learners, particularly boys, are more likely to be labelled as disruptive and face higher rates of exclusion. This undermines their sense of belonging and creates a cycle of underachievement. Conversely, lower expectations for some ethnic groups can lead to less challenging work, limiting their progress.

- School culture and identity: A school culture that doesn't actively celebrate diversity can alienate learners from minority backgrounds. This might manifest in a lack of recognition for cultural events, dress codes that conflict with religious practices, or limited support for learners facing racism. Learners who feel their identity is overlooked or marginalised are less likely to develop a strong connection to their school.

- Peer relationships and discrimination: Experiencing or witnessing racism and discrimination – whether from peers or within the wider community – can make learners feel unsafe and undervalued. This erodes their confidence and impacts academic outcomes. Social dynamics, such as being part of a small minority in a predominantly White school, can exacerbate feelings of isolation.

- Parental engagement: Families from minority ethnic backgrounds may feel disconnected from the education system, particularly if there are language barriers or a perceived lack of understanding of their needs. This can reduce the effectiveness of home-school partnerships, which are crucial for learner success.

What can we do to narrow the ethnicity gap?

Ethnicity gaps are not inevitable. Here are some practical suggestions for tackling the gaps:

Firstly, we can create a culturally inclusive curriculum. In practice, this might involve incorporating diverse voices and perspectives across all subjects. For example, we might teach learners about Black British history alongside a traditional focus on kings and wars, and we might introduce learners to literature from a range of different cultures. We might also highlight the contributions of scientists, artists, and leaders from diverse backgrounds to inspire learners and validate their experiences.

Secondly, we can train staff to recognise and challenge bias. This might involve providing regular training on unconscious bias to ensure teachers set high expectations for all learners and challenge stereotypes. It might also involve equipping staff with the skills to address racist incidents sensitively and effectively, fostering an inclusive environment.

Thirdly, we can actively celebrate diversity. In practice, we might mark cultural and religious events such as Diwali, Eid, or Black History Month, demonstrating respect and valuing learners' identities. We might also create safe spaces for learners to express their heritage and share their experiences, helping them feel seen and heard.

Fourthly, we might encourage diverse leadership and role models by recruiting and supporting teachers and leaders from a range of ethnic backgrounds. Seeing people like themselves in positions of authority can help inspire learners and reinforce a sense of belonging. We might also invite guest speakers from minority communities to share their successes and insights with learners.

Fifthly, we can build stronger links with families by offering language support and tailored workshops for parents from minority backgrounds to improve engagement with their children's education. We might also work with community leaders to bridge gaps and develop trust between schools and families.

Finally, we can tackle racism proactively by implementing clear anti-racism policies and ensure all learners and staff understand them, and by monitoring incidents of discrimination and taking swift, meaningful action to prevent recurrence.

The ethnicity attainment gap is not just about academic ability – it is deeply connected to a learner's sense of inclusion and belonging within their school. Schools that embrace diversity, tackle bias, and celebrate every learner's identity can foster environments where all children feel valued and empowered to succeed. By doing so, we can ensure that no child's potential is limited by their ethnicity.

Self-evaluation

Having read about the ethnicity gap, put the theory into practice by answering the following self-evaluative questions:

1. What are the key factors contributing to the ethnicity attainment gap?
2. How do socio-economic factors intersect with ethnicity to influence academic outcomes?
3. Which groups have shown significant improvements in attainment over the years, and what factors have contributed to this progress?
4. Why do Gypsy, Roma, and Traveller learners continue to face persistent challenges in closing the attainment gap?
5. How can you implement a culturally inclusive curriculum to address the ethnicity attainment gap effectively?
6. What role does teacher bias play in shaping academic outcomes for learners, and how can it be addressed?
7. How can the strategies mentioned in this chapter (e.g., mentorship, parental engagement, anti-bias training) be combined to create a holistic approach to narrowing the ethnicity gap?
8. Which specific intervention or strategy mentioned here do you believe would have the most immediate impact on reducing disparities, and why?
9. If you were responsible for developing a school policy to address the attainment gap, which recommendations from the text would you prioritise?
10. How can the education system continue to adapt to ensure sustained progress in narrowing the ethnicity gap over the next decade?

6 The SEND gap

As well as gender and ethnicity, special educational needs and disabilities (SEND) have long accounted for significant attainment gaps. The SEND gap is a persistent challenge in education and highlights inequalities in support, resources, and opportunities for SEND learners.

Learners with SEND often achieve significantly lower outcomes than their peers at every stage of education. For example:

- At Key Stage 2, in 2022 only 22% of learners with an Education, Health and Care Plan (EHCP) met the expected standard in reading, writing, and maths, compared to 59% of all learners. For learners receiving SEND support (but without an EHCP), the figure was 30%.

- At GCSE, in 2022 26.7% of learners with SEND achieved a grade 4 or above in GCSE English and maths, compared to 71.1% of their non-SEND peers. Among learners with an Education, Health and Care Plan (EHCP), this figure dropped to just 17.9%.

- At Post-16, learners with SEND are significantly less likely to progress to Level 3 qualifications, with only 18% of learners with SEND continuing to A levels or equivalent courses, compared to 45% of non-SEND learners. Learners with SEND are then much less likely to achieve Level 3 qualifications and are more likely to be in lower-paid or insecure jobs after leaving school.

- Learners with SEND accounted for 42% of all permanent exclusions and 40% of all fixed-term exclusions, despite making up only 15% of the school population.

While there have been some improvements in the education and inclusion of learners with SEND, the attainment gap has remained stubbornly persistent over the past two decades.

In the early 2000s, the percentage of SEND learners achieving the expected standards was even lower than today. However, while non-SEND learners have seen consistent improvements in attainment, the progress for SEND learners has been slower, resulting in the gap remaining wide. For example, the introduction of the Special Educational Needs and Disability (SEND) Code of Practice in 2015 aimed to provide clearer support frameworks, but its impact on attainment has been limited due to challenges in implementation and funding.

Changes to the curriculum and assessment methods, such as the shift from modular GCSEs to linear exams, have disproportionately affected SEND learners. Many rely on continuous assessment and coursework to demonstrate their abilities, which do not feature as prominently in the current system.

Funding for SEND provision has not kept pace with demand. Over the last 20 years, increasing numbers of learners have been identified as needing SEND support, but many schools report insufficient resources to meet these needs effectively.

The pandemic further widened the attainment gap, as many SEND learners struggled with access to specialised support during school closures. Online learning environments often lacked the necessary adaptations, leaving these learners at a disadvantage.

Exclusion rates for SEND learners remain disproportionately high, with little improvement over the years. This suggests that behaviour policies still fail to adequately account for the challenges faced by SEND learners, such as sensory sensitivities or difficulties with emotional regulation.

The data suggest that, while there have been pockets of improvement, the fundamental issues underpinning the SEND attainment gap remain unresolved. Progress is probably being hindered by:

- Insufficient funding, which limits the availability of specialist resources
- Inconsistent implementation of policies across schools and local authorities
- Systemic barriers, such as a one-size-fits-all curriculum and assessment model

One of the complications is that the SEND gap – like the ethnicity gap – is influenced by a range of interrelated factors, including systemic challenges, resource constraints, and attitudinal barriers, such as:

- Delayed identification and support: Many SEND learners are not identified early enough, leading to delays in providing the tailored support they need. Even when SEND is identified, bureaucratic delays in securing EHCPs can result in learners missing critical interventions during key parts of their learning journeys.
- Inadequate resources: Schools often struggle to provide high-quality support due to limited funding, staffing shortages, and inadequate staff training. Specialist services such as speech and language therapy or educational psychology are often oversubscribed, leading to long waiting times.
- Mainstream inclusion challenges: While the principle of inclusion is widely supported, many mainstream schools lack the expertise or resources to effectively

meet the needs of SEND learners. SEND learners in mainstream settings may face bullying, isolation, or teaching that is not suitably adapted to their needs, leaving them disengaged.

- Exclusion rates: Learners with SEND are disproportionately represented in school exclusions data. In 2021, they accounted for 42% of permanent exclusions, often for behaviours linked to their unmet needs. Exclusions, naturally, disrupt learning and exacerbate attainment gaps.
- Low expectations and bias: Some educators may hold unconscious biases about the abilities and capabilities of SEND learners, leading to lower expectations and limited access to challenging work. SEND learners may also internalise these low expectations, reducing their confidence and ambition.
- Transitions and continuity: Transitions between school phases, or from school to further education or employment, are particularly challenging for SEND learners, leading to gaps in support and reduced attainment.

Closing the SEND gap therefore requires systemic change, increased investment, and cultural shifts within schools. This might include:

1. Early identification and intervention – achieved by training teachers to recognise early signs of SEND and implement classroom-based interventions while awaiting formal assessments, and by investing in screening tools and resources to support early identification, particularly in the early years

2. Improved EHCP processes – achieved by streamlining the EHCP process to reduce waiting times and ensure that learners receive timely and appropriate support, and by monitoring the implementation of EHCPs to ensure that the agreed provision is delivered consistently

3. Specialist training for teachers – achieved by providing ongoing professional development to equip teachers with strategies to differentiate teaching and manage diverse learning needs, and by promoting the use of evidence-based approaches, such as task-scaffolding and assistive technology, to support SEND learners in mainstream settings

4. Increased funding and resources – achieved by allocating sufficient funding to mainstream schools to hire additional staff, such as teaching assistants or SEND specialists, and to help them access external services, as well as by expanding the availability of alternative provision and special schools for learners with more complex needs

5. Inclusive classroom practices – achieved by ensuring that teaching methods, materials, and assessments are accessible to all learners, and by fostering a classroom culture of empathy and respect, encouraging all learners to value diversity and support their peers

6. Reducing exclusions – achieved by developing proactive behaviour policies that address the underlying causes of challenging behaviour, such as sensory overload or unmet needs, and by providing staff with de-escalation training and alternative strategies to manage behaviour positively

7. Improving transitions – achieved by establishing robust transition plans to support SEND learners as they move between school phases or into further education or work, and by involving learners and their families in planning these transitions to ensure that their needs are fully understood and met

8. Parental and learner voice – achieved by engaging families as partners in their children's education, ensuring that they feel informed and empowered to advocate for their needs, and by regularly seeking feedback from SEND learners about their experiences and then using this to inform school practices

The SEND attainment gap is a symptom of broader inequalities in the education system. While it cannot be closed overnight, progress is possible through targeted interventions, adequate funding, and more inclusive practices. By prioritising the needs of SEND learners, schools can ensure that every child has the opportunity to succeed, regardless of their starting point. This is not just about meeting statutory obligations; it's about creating an education system that works for all.

How the SEND gap intersects with inclusion and belonging

Here are some ways in which the SEND gap intersects with our theme of inclusion and belonging . . .

- Classroom integration: In inclusive classrooms, SEND learners feel like equal members of the learning community. However, when lessons are not differentiated or teaching assistants are over-relied upon, SEND learners may feel separated from their peers, reducing their sense of belonging and engagement. For example, learners frequently withdrawn from mainstream lessons for individual support may feel stigmatised, which can affect their confidence and willingness to participate in group learning activities.

- Peer relationships: A strong sense of belonging is fostered by positive peer interactions. Learners with SEND who experience bullying or social exclusion may feel isolated, which can undermine their emotional well-being and academic performance. Schools with a culture of empathy and understanding, where learners are taught to celebrate differences, report better outcomes for SEND learners.

- Teacher attitudes and expectations: The way teachers perceive and interact with SEND learners has a profound effect on their sense of inclusion. High expectations coupled with tailored support can help SEND learners feel capable and valued. However, unconscious biases or low expectations can make SEND learners feel 'othered', limiting their opportunities to access the full curriculum and fulfil their potential.

- Accessibility and adaptations: Learners with SEND often struggle in environments that are not designed with their needs in mind. A lack of accessible resources, such as visual aids, assistive technology, or sensory-friendly spaces, can make learning feel exclusionary. When schools create an environment where all learners, including those with SEND, can participate equitably, they reinforce learners' sense of belonging.

- Parental and learner voice: Schools that actively involve SEND learners and their families in decision-making demonstrate respect and inclusion. When SEND learners feel heard, they are more likely to engage in their own education. Conversely, schools that overlook or dismiss the input of SEND learners risk alienating them, which can negatively impact their motivation and academic outcomes.

What can we do to narrow the SEND gap?

As with all attainment gaps, the SEND gap can be narrowed, if not closed, with deliberate action. Here are some suggestions:

Firstly, we can adopt inclusive teaching practices, such as adaptive or responsive teaching including the use of task-scaffolding, in order to ensure that all learners can access and engage with the same ambitious curriculum as their non-SEND peers. We might also incorporate collaborative learning opportunities that encourage peer interaction and teamwork.

Secondly, we can cultivate an inclusive school culture, such as by celebrating diversity and promoting awareness and understanding of SEND through assemblies, workshops, and peer-led initiatives. We can train staff and learners to recognise and challenge discrimination or bullying related to SEND.

Thirdly, we can provide emotional and social support, such as creating safe spaces, as well as sensory rooms or quiet zones, where SEND learners can regulate their emotions, and we can introduce buddy systems or peer mentoring to help SEND learners feel more connected and supported.

Fourthly, we can enhance accessibility by investing in assistive technologies and resources that empower SEND learners to engage with learning on their terms, and by ensuring that the physical environment is accommodating, with features like wheelchair-accessible facilities and clear signage.

Finally, we can involve families and learners in decision-making by regularly consulting with parents and carers to understand the unique needs of SEND learners and involve them in setting targets and planning interventions, and by listening to the voices of SEND learners, valuing their insights and experiences to shape policies and practices that truly meet their needs.

The SEND attainment gap is not – or at least not solely – a matter of academic ability; rather, it is deeply intertwined with whether learners feel included and whether they feel they belong in their school community. If we can embrace diversity, celebrate individual strengths, and invest in more inclusive practices, we can help SEND learners reach their full potential. Ultimately, fostering a sense of belonging is not just about improving academic outcomes; it is about creating a school environment where every child feels they matter.

Self-evaluation

Having read about the SEND gap, put the theory into practice by answering the following self-evaluative questions:

1. Can you summarise the key factors contributing to the SEND attainment gap in education?
2. How do the statistics provided about SEND learners' performance at Key Stage 2, GCSE, and Post-16 highlight the challenges they face?
3. What systemic and resource-related challenges are identified as barriers to closing the SEND gap?
4. How has the implementation of the SEND Code of Practice influenced the attainment gap, and what are the main limitations of this policy?
5. How does this chapter describe the intersection of the SEND gap with inclusion and belonging in schools?
6. How do teacher attitudes and expectations impact the inclusion and sense of belonging for SEND learners?
7. Which of the suggested actions for narrowing the SEND gap could you or your school implement immediately?
8. How do your current classroom practices foster a sense of belonging for SEND learners? Are there areas where you could improve?
9. Does this chapter advocate for equity or equality in addressing the SEND gap, and how do the proposed solutions align with this perspective?
10. Which systemic changes mentioned in this chapter do you believe are most critical for closing the SEND attainment gap, and why?

7 The socio-economic gap

Moving on, the socio-economic gap manifests in learners who live in poverty achieving lower outcomes at school, reduced rates of progression to further education, and limited career opportunities and earnings potential.

Here's some supporting data . . .

In Early Years, in 2022, by the age of 5, only 57% of disadvantaged learners had achieved a 'good level of development' at the end of the Early Years Foundation Stage, compared to 74% of their more affluent peers.

At Key Stage 2, also in 2022, at the end of primary school, just 43% of disadvantaged learners achieved the expected standard in reading, writing, and maths, compared to 65% of non-disadvantaged learners. This represents a gap of 22 percentage points.

At GCSE, in 2022, the gap in GCSE attainment was starker still: Just 29% of disadvantaged learners achieved a strong pass (grades 9–5) in English and maths, compared to 57% of their more affluent peers. The average Attainment 8 score (which measures performance across eight qualifications) was 37.5 for disadvantaged learners versus 52.3 for non-disadvantaged learners.

Post-16, disadvantaged learners are significantly less likely to progress to further education or university. For example: In 2020, 26% of learners eligible for free school meals (FSM) entered higher education by age 19, compared to 45% of their non-FSM peers. FSM learners are less likely to attend top-tier universities, too, with only 2.4% attending a Russell Group university, compared to 10.9% of non-FSM learners.

There has been modest improvement in closing the socio-economic gap over the past two decades. For example: In 2003, the GCSE attainment gap was around 28 percentage points; by 2022, it had narrowed to 20 percentage points for strong passes in English and maths. Early Years and Key Stage 2 outcomes have also improved slightly. But the socio-economic gap remains stubbornly wide, particularly in areas of high deprivation.

The Covid-19 pandemic widened the attainment gap in many areas, reversing some of the progress made in the years immediately preceding it, because disadvantaged learners were disproportionately affected by school closures, not least because they had more limited access to the technology needed to access remote learning and were much less likely to have parental support or a suitable place to study at home. In 2021, estimates suggested that the gap had grown by as much as 0.5 months of learning for primary learners and 0.8 months for secondary learners.

It's worth noting that the socio-economic gap is more pronounced in some regions than others. For example, disadvantaged learners in the North East and in Yorkshire and the Humber often face larger gaps compared to their peers in London, where targeted interventions such as the London Challenge had a positive impact.

Despite targeted funding, such as the Pupil Premium which was introduced in 2011, progress in narrowing the gap has been slower than anticipated. Challenges such as entrenched poverty, limited access to resources, and regional inequalities continue to hamper efforts, as do changes to the benefits system and changes to the way we measure outcomes.

If we are to learn from these data, to further close the socio-economic attainment gap, we must:

- Focus on early intervention, particularly in the Early Years and Key Stage 1
- Ensure effective use of the Pupil Premium Grant and other sources of disadvantage funding by investing in evidence-based strategies such as tutoring and literacy programmes
- Address regional disparities by disproportionately targeting support to areas of higher deprivation
- Provide enhanced pastoral care and mental health support to help disadvantaged learners overcome the long-term effects of the pandemic and of the cost-of-living crisis

Why does the socio-economic attainment gap exist?

There are several reasons for the socio-economic gap's existence, including:

- *Material poverty*: Learners from disadvantaged backgrounds may lack access to resources such as books, a quiet place to study, or reliable internet, which are essential for supporting learning outside of school. Economic insecurity can lead to housing instability, hunger, or poor health, all of which negatively impact a child's ability to focus and thrive in school.
- *Parental engagement*: Parents from lower socio-economic backgrounds may face barriers to supporting their child's education, such as time constraints due to work, lower confidence in engaging with schools, or language barriers. Differences in parental expectations can also contribute, with disadvantaged families sometimes less aware of or able to navigate pathways to higher education and career opportunities.

- **School resources**: Schools in deprived areas often face additional challenges, including higher rates of staff turnover, fewer resources, and a greater concentration of learners with complex needs. This can lead to larger class sizes, fewer extracurricular opportunities, and less targeted support.

- **Cultural capital**: Disadvantaged learners may have fewer opportunities to build cultural capital – the knowledge, experiences, and skills valued by the education system and society. For example, they may have limited access to museums, theatre trips, or enrichment activities that contribute to academic success.

- **Aspirations and motivation**: Economic hardship can lead to lower aspirations and self-belief among disadvantaged learners. A lack of role models who have succeeded through education may reinforce feelings that academic success is unattainable or irrelevant.

What can we do to close the gap?

The socio-economic gap may be significant and stubborn, but it is certainly not insurmountable. Here are some ways in which we can begin to narrow the gap . . .

Firstly, we can ensure that funding such as the Pupil Premium is used strategically to invest in evidence-based interventions. This might include tutoring, literacy programmes, or subsidising extracurricular activities. We should then monitor the impact of this funding and ensure it directly benefits disadvantaged learners.

Secondly, we can provide early intervention. Support should begin in the Early Years Foundation Stage to ensure that all children develop the foundational skills needed for future success. High-quality early education is especially important for narrowing the gap at its source. We can also invest in family support programmes that help parents engage in their child's education from an early age.

Thirdly, we can invest in high-quality teaching for all. This means prioritising professional development to ensure all teachers are equipped to deliver differentiated instruction for diverse needs. Specialist programmes, such as literacy and numeracy catch-up sessions, can help disadvantaged learners keep pace with their peers.

Fourthly, we can address the broader challenges faced by disadvantaged learners by investing in mental health and well-being services. This includes access to school counsellors, mentoring programmes, and breakfast clubs. We can create a school culture where every learner feels supported and valued, boosting their confidence and engagement.

Fifthly, we can provide all learners with opportunities to experience cultural enrichment. This could involve free trips, guest speakers, or partnerships with local organisations. We should also encourage participation in extracurricular activities, ensuring financial barriers do not exclude disadvantaged learners.

Sixthly, we can offer workshops or resources that help parents understand how to support their child's learning at home. We can use outreach strategies to engage hard-to-reach families, including home visits or translation services for non-English-speaking parents.

Finally, we can expose learners to a wide range of careers and higher education opportunities through trips, careers fairs, and talks from relatable role models. We might offer personalised career and academic guidance that helps disadvantaged learners map out a clear pathway to success.

The socio-economic gap is a complex and persistent challenge in education, but by addressing the root causes – poverty, a lack of resources, deficits in cultural capital, and limited aspirations – and by implementing targeted, evidence-based strategies, we can help to level the playing field. Ensuring every child, regardless of affluence and social class, has access to high-quality education is not just an ethical imperative but a practical necessity for building a fairer and more prosperous society. When people from every background have the chance to contribute their skills to society, we all benefit.

How the socio-economic gap intersects inclusion and belonging

As we've seen, learners who feel they belong at school are more likely to participate actively in learning, develop positive relationships with teachers and peers, and persevere in the face of challenges. What's more, a strong sense of belonging can mitigate some of the barriers disadvantaged learners face, such as low self-esteem or lack of confidence.

Talking of barriers, disadvantaged learners may feel out of place if the school environment predominantly reflects middle-class norms, values, or cultural references. This can manifest in the curriculum, extracurricular activities, or even everyday interactions.

Learners eligible for free school meals or other forms of support may also feel stigmatised or labelled as 'different', leading to feelings of isolation.

Economic barriers can exclude disadvantaged learners from fully participating in school life, such as joining clubs, attending trips, or accessing resources, which further reinforces a sense of exclusion.

When learners feel they do not belong, they are less likely to engage with learning or see school as a pathway to success. This can lead to higher absenteeism, lower motivation, and, ultimately, poorer outcomes, widening the socio-economic attainment gap.

We might tackle these barriers by:

1. **Building positive relationships.** Teachers play a critical role in creating a welcoming environment. By showing genuine care and high expectations for all learners, we can build trust and a sense of value. Mentoring programmes can provide disadvantaged learners with role models who understand and can support their unique challenges.

2. ***Creating an inclusive curriculum.*** We should ensure the curriculum reflects diverse perspectives and experiences, allowing all learners to see themselves represented in their learning. We should also avoid assumptions about learners' background knowledge or experiences and provide context where needed to ensure fair access to learning for all.

3. ***Removing economic barriers.*** We could subsidise or cover the costs for school trips, uniform, and extracurricular activities to ensure disadvantaged learners can participate fully – and poverty proof our school wherever possible. We could also provide access to resources like laptops, books, and internet connectivity so all learners can engage in homework and independent study.

4. ***Combatting stigma.*** We should avoid practices that single out disadvantaged learners, such as overtly identifying those receiving free school meals. Instead, we should use discreet and universal approaches to support learners in need. We should also try to foster a culture of mutual respect and empathy by educating all learners about diversity, inclusion, and the importance of supporting one another.

5. ***Celebrating diversity.*** We should try to highlight and celebrate the contributions of learners from all backgrounds, ensuring their achievements and identities are recognised and valued. And we could use assemblies, projects, and events to showcase the rich variety of cultures, languages, and traditions within our school community.

6. ***Engaging families.*** We could build strong relationships with parents and carers from disadvantaged backgrounds, offering workshops, home visits, or tailored support to help them feel included in their child's education. We could provide accessible communication and opportunities for families to contribute to school life.

The socio-economic gap is deeply influenced by whether learners feel a sense of inclusion and belonging in their school environment. By fostering an inclusive culture, removing barriers to participation, and building strong relationships, we can help disadvantaged learners feel valued and engaged. This, in turn, will boost their confidence, motivation, and achievements, helping to narrow the attainment gap and create a more equitable education system. Every child deserves to feel they belong, and when they do, the benefits can be profound – not just for the individual but for the whole school community.

Self-evaluation

Having read about the socio-economic gap, put the theory into practice by answering the following self-evaluative questions:

1. How well do I understand the factors contributing to the socio-economic attainment gap?

2. What key statistics from this chapter stand out to me, and how do they illustrate the persistence of the socio-economic gap?

3. Which of the proposed interventions for narrowing the socio-economic gap do I find most compelling, and why?

4. What insights have I gained about the importance of early intervention in addressing educational disparities?

5. How has my understanding of the impact of the Covid-19 pandemic on disadvantaged learners changed after reading this chapter?

6. How can fostering a sense of inclusion and belonging in schools address the socio-economic attainment gap?

7. Which strategies outlined in this chapter could I apply in my own school, and what challenges might I face in doing so?

8. How has the discussion of regional disparities informed my perspective on tackling educational inequality?

9. In what ways can I build stronger relationships with disadvantaged learners to help them feel supported and valued?

10. What are three concrete steps I can take, based on this text, to contribute to closing the socio-economic attainment gap?

8 The vulnerable children gap

The attainment gap for looked after children (children in care) and other vulnerable learners is among the widest because these children often face unique challenges that significantly impact their academic outcomes. Closing this gap requires a coordinated approach that addresses their specific needs and ensures they have the same opportunities as their peers to succeed in school and beyond.

On average, looked after children perform significantly worse than their peers at every stage of education:

- In 2022, only 26% of looked after children achieved a pass in English and maths at GCSE, compared to 58% of non-looked after peers.

- The progress score for looked after children at Key Stage 4 was −1.23 in 2022, indicating they are falling behind their peers in academic growth.

Looked after children are also less likely to pursue further education. Only 13% of care leavers progress to university by age 19, compared to around 43% of all young people.

Children with Child Protection Plans or those categorised as 'in need' often face similarly poor outcomes, highlighting the broader vulnerabilities beyond formal care status.

Here's a deeper dive into the data . . .

In 2022, only 49% of looked after children achieved a 'good level of development' at the end of the Early Years Foundation Stage, compared to 72% of all learners. Vulnerable children (those on Child Protection Plans or identified as 'in need') also performed significantly below average.

At Key Stage 2 in 2022, 37% of looked after children met the expected standard in reading, writing, and maths, compared to 59% of all learners. Children in need performed similarly, with just 38% meeting the expected standard.

At GCSE in 2022, only 26% of looked after children achieved a grade 4 or above (a standard pass) in English and maths, compared to 58% of all learners. The gap widens further when considering Progress 8 scores, which measure academic growth: Looked after children had an average score of −1.23 compared to −0.26 for all learners; other vulnerable children performed similarly poorly, with fewer than 30% achieving a pass in English and maths.

Only 13% of care leavers progress to university by age 19, compared to around 43% of all learners. Even fewer attend top-tier institutions, with less than 2% of care leavers enrolling in a Russell Group university.

Looked after children are more likely to miss school, with attendance rates significantly below the national average. They are also disproportionately represented in exclusion statistics. In 2022, looked after children were five times more likely to be excluded than their peers.

Over the last two decades, there have been some modest improvements in the attainment of looked after children, particularly in primary education. For example, in 2005, only 28% of looked after children achieved the expected standard in Key Stage 2 reading, writing, and maths, compared to 37% in 2022.

At GCSE, progress has been slower. In 2003, only 11% of looked after children achieved a pass in English and maths. By 2022, this figure had risen to 26%, but the gap remains significant.

University attendance for care leavers has increased slightly over the past 20 years, from around 6% in the early 2000s to 13% today. However, this is still far below the national average of over 40%.

Despite targeted interventions such as the introduction of Virtual School Heads in 2014 and the statutory Personal Education Plans (PEPs), the attainment gap has remained stubbornly wide. The challenges of instability, trauma, and low expectations have proven difficult to overcome, particularly for older children.

The Covid-19 pandemic exacerbated existing disparities. Looked after and vulnerable children were disproportionately affected by school closures and limited access to technology, leading to further learning loss.

While there have been incremental improvements over the last 20 years, the attainment gap for looked after and other vulnerable children remains a significant issue. These children continue to face barriers that hinder their progress, and although policies and interventions have helped, the pace of change has been slow.

The vulnerable children gap exists because:

- Many looked after children experience instability, such as frequent changes in foster placements or residential homes. This often leads to school moves, disrupting their education and making it difficult to build relationships or maintain consistent progress.

- Children in care are more likely to have experienced abuse, neglect, or family breakdown. These adverse experiences can lead to emotional and behavioural difficulties, impacting their ability to focus and thrive in school. High levels of anxiety or stress may result in increased absenteeism or disengagement from learning.

- Vulnerable children often lack the stable and supportive relationships that many of their peers take for granted. Limited parental involvement or advocacy can mean their educational needs are not prioritised.
- There is sometimes an unconscious bias among educators, social workers, or carers that leads to lower expectations for looked after and vulnerable children. This can limit the opportunities they are given to excel.
- Frequent school moves, lack of access to resources like books or technology, and disruptions caused by court appearances or social work meetings can all detract from their ability to keep up academically.

To combat this, we might:

1. **Provide stable schooling**: Local authorities and schools should prioritise minimising school moves for looked after children, even when placement changes occur. Schools should develop robust transition plans to ensure continuity of learning and support when moves are unavoidable.

2. **Ensure high-quality teaching**: High-quality teaching is crucial for closing all attainment gaps but has a disproportionately positive impact on disadvantaged and vulnerable children such as those in care. We should therefore invest in professional development to ensure teachers understand how to meet the needs of looked after and vulnerable children. High quality teaching should then be supported by small-group interventions, one-to-one tutoring, and targeted support to help learners catch up and stay on track.

3. **Appoint designated teachers**: Every school is required to have a Designated Teacher for Looked After Children. This individual should champion the needs of these learners, coordinate their Personal Education Plans (PEPs), and act as a key point of contact for social workers and carers. For the role to be effective, however, we need to ensure the designated teacher receives adequate training and resources.

4. **Provide emotional and pastoral support**: We should invest in school-based counselling services and mentoring programmes to help children process trauma and develop resilience. We should create a nurturing school environment where learners feel safe, supported, and valued.

5. **Raise expectations and aspirations**: We should foster high expectations for looked after and vulnerable children, encouraging them to aim for ambitious goals. We also need to expose these learners to a wide range of opportunities, including university visits, career talks, and enrichment activities, to broaden their horizons.

6. **Enhance collaboration**: Schools, local authorities, and social care teams must work closely together to coordinate support. Regular communication ensures that children's educational needs are considered alongside their welfare. We need to

engage carers and families in a child's education, providing them with resources and support to help at home.

7. **Monitor and support attendance**: We should address absenteeism through early intervention and tailored support plans. For example, we could offer flexible timetables or alternative provision for learners who struggle with the traditional school day.

How the vulnerable children gap intersects with inclusion and belonging

For looked after children and other vulnerable children, a sense of inclusion and belonging in school is not just desirable; it is essential.

These children often face unique challenges that affect their ability to engage in learning. When they feel valued and included, they are more likely to succeed academically. Conversely, feelings of exclusion or alienation can widen the already significant attainment gap.

Many looked after and vulnerable children have experienced trauma, neglect, or instability. This can lead to feelings of distrust or low self-worth, making it harder for them to build connections with teachers and peers. A sense of belonging can help to mitigate the emotional impact of these experiences, giving children a foundation of stability and safety from which to learn.

Without a strong sense of belonging, children may disengage from school. This can manifest as poor attendance, disruptive behaviour, or lack of motivation – all of which contribute to the attainment gap. Feeling excluded can lead to a self-perpetuating cycle: Disengagement leads to lower achievement, which in turn reinforces feelings of inadequacy.

Looked after and vulnerable children are often aware of being 'different'. Whether it's through labelling, unconscious bias, or being treated differently, this can exacerbate feelings of exclusion. Stigma undermines their confidence and willingness to participate fully in school life.

We can tackle the vulnerable children gap by:

1. **Building relationships.** Positive, trusting relationships with adults in school are critical. When teachers show genuine care and have high expectations, children feel valued and are more likely to engage. Mentoring programmes can provide consistent support from a trusted adult, helping children feel connected and motivated.

2. **Creating a welcoming environment.** We can foster a sense of belonging by ensuring that looked after and vulnerable children are fully integrated into school life. This includes celebrating their achievements, involving them in extracurricular activities, and ensuring they have access to the same opportunities as their peers.

3. **Adapting the curriculum.** An inclusive curriculum that reflects diverse experiences and perspectives helps children see themselves in what they're learning. Schools

should therefore be mindful of how content is presented to avoid reinforcing feelings of exclusion.

4. **Tackling stigma.** Normalising support services and avoiding practices that single out vulnerable children (e.g. public identification of looked after children) can reduce stigma. Whole-school education about diversity and inclusion helps create a culture of empathy and respect.

5. *Involving learners in decision-making.* Allowing children to have a voice in their education fosters a sense of ownership and belonging. For example, involving them in the creation of Personal Education Plans (PEPs) ensures their perspectives are heard and valued.

Further, it's important to note that frequent school or placement moves are common for looked after children and can disrupt their sense of belonging. Schools can mitigate this by ensuring smooth transitions, maintaining consistent support, and prioritising stability wherever possible. In practice, this might mean:

- Appointing a designated teacher: As I've said, every school must have a designated teacher for looked after children who advocates for their needs and ensures they feel included.
- Providing emotional support: Invest in pastoral care, such as school counsellors or peer mentoring schemes, to help children process emotions and build resilience.
- Focusing on peer relationships: Encourage group work, buddy systems, and inclusive play to help children form friendships and feel part of the school community.
- Offering tailored interventions: One-to-one tuition or small-group support can help children catch up academically, building their confidence and sense of achievement.
- Engaging parents and families: Schools should work closely with foster carers, social workers, and families to provide a consistent approach to support.

For looked after and vulnerable children, a sense of inclusion and belonging is a powerful antidote to the challenges they face. When children feel accepted, valued, and supported within their school, they are more likely to engage, persevere, and succeed. Narrowing the attainment gap is about more than academic interventions; it's about creating a school culture where every child knows they matter.

Self-evaluation

Having read about the vulnerable learner gap, put the theory into practice by answering the following self-evaluative questions:

1. How well do I understand the key reasons behind the attainment gap for looked after children and other vulnerable learners?

2. Can I identify the key statistics and data points that highlight the disparity in educational outcomes for looked after children compared to their peers?

3. What are the unique challenges faced by looked after children, and how do they affect their academic performance and emotional well-being?

4. How do interventions like the Personal Education Plan (PEP) and Virtual School Heads aim to improve outcomes for vulnerable children?

5. What strategies can I suggest to ensure looked after children experience greater stability in their schooling and avoid frequent school moves?

6. How can I contribute to creating a more inclusive school culture that helps vulnerable children feel a sense of belonging and reduces stigma?

7. In what ways can I help raise expectations for looked after children and ensure high-quality teaching tailored to their specific needs?

8. How can schools and social care teams work better together to meet the needs of vulnerable children? What role can I play in this collaboration?

9. How can we better address the emotional and mental health needs of looked after children to ensure they are ready to engage in their education?

10. What methods should I use to monitor the progress and well-being of vulnerable children, ensuring that tailored interventions are effective and sustained?

9 The mobility gap

Service children – those with parents in the Armed Forces – and other learners who experience high levels of mobility face a unique set of challenges in education. Frequent school moves, interruptions to learning, and the emotional toll of their circumstances often result in an attainment gap compared to their peers. Addressing this gap requires tailored strategies that provide continuity, support, and stability.

Let's look at service children first . . .

Service children often perform below their peers, particularly in secondary education, as a result of disrupted schooling and the emotional impact of parental deployment. At Key Stage 2, service children's attainment in reading, writing, and maths is generally on par with their peers, but by Key Stage 4, they tend to fall behind. In 2022, 34% of service children achieved a strong pass (grade 5 or above) in English and maths GCSE, compared to 50% of all learners.

As for other highly mobile learners, children who frequently move schools – for example, those from Traveller families or families in temporary housing – are more likely to struggle academically. Research shows that mobility disrupts continuity in education, with mobile learners achieving lower GCSE results and being more likely to leave education without qualifications.

So, why – specifically – do highly mobile learners perform worse at school?

Firstly, service children and highly mobile learners often move between schools multiple times during their education. Each move can disrupt their learning, making it harder to build on prior knowledge and establish relationships with teachers and peers. Inconsistent curricula, teaching methods, and assessment standards across schools exacerbate these challenges.

Secondly, service children may face stress or anxiety due to parental deployment, family separation, or concerns for their parents' safety. Mobile learners often experience social isolation and struggle to feel a sense of belonging in new schools.

Thirdly, vulnerable children often lose access to tailored support when they move schools. This is particularly problematic for children with special educational needs or those receiving pastoral care.

Frequent moves can also lead to gaps or delays in transferring school records, making it harder for teachers to understand and meet a child's needs. And mobile learners may be perceived as "disruptive" or "unreliable" by peers or staff, leading to lower expectations and reduced opportunities to succeed.

What does the data tell us?

In the Early Years Foundation Stage, service children generally perform in line with their peers. At Key Stage 2, 70% of service children met the expected standard in reading, writing, and maths in 2022, slightly below the 73% national average. At GCSE, only 34% of service children achieved a strong pass (grade 5 or above) in English and maths in 2022, compared to 50% of all learners. Their Progress 8 scores, which measure academic growth, were −0.19 compared to the national average of −0.03, highlighting slower progress. Service children are less likely to enter higher education, with participation rates around 33%, compared to 43% of all learners. Only a small proportion pursue further study in competitive fields, though there has been a slight upward trend in recent years.

Highly mobile learners, meanwhile, are twice as likely as their peers to leave school without qualifications. Highly mobile learners have lower attendance rates, often below 85%, compared to the average of around 95% for all learners. Disengagement is more common, with higher exclusion rates and lower participation in extracurricular activities.

In the early 2000s, service children often lagged further behind their peers, particularly in primary education. For example, in 2005, only 50% of service children met the expected standard at Key Stage 2, compared to 70% in 2022. This improvement reflects better targeted support, including the introduction of the Service Pupil Premium (SPP) in 2011. At GCSE level, the attainment gap for service children has narrowed slightly but remains significant. In 2003, fewer than 20% of service children achieved a strong pass in English and maths, compared to 34% today. Progress has been inconsistent, with gaps widening in some years due to factors such as curriculum changes and the pandemic. Covid-19 disproportionately affected service families, particularly those stationed overseas or in areas with limited access to remote learning. This has widened the gap in some cases, highlighting the ongoing challenges of mobility and access.

The attainment gap for highly mobile learners has remained stubbornly wide over the last two decades. Improvements in data tracking and transfer systems have helped reduce some of the disruptions caused by frequent moves, but these gains have been uneven across regions and schools. Despite efforts to address the needs of mobile learners, such as through the Fair Access Protocol, outcomes have not improved significantly for many groups, particularly those from Traveller families or in temporary housing.

In sum, while the attainment gap for service children has narrowed modestly over the last 20 years, particularly at Key Stage 2, progress at GCSE and beyond remains slow. For highly mobile learners, the gap has proven more persistent, reflecting the complex and multifaceted barriers they face. Addressing these challenges requires sustained effort, targeted funding, and a focus on ensuring continuity and inclusion in education.

How can we close the mobility gap?

Here are some practical suggestions for tackling the mobility gap . . .

1. *Provide more continuity in learning*: We could use portable learning tools such as online platforms to ensure continuity of education between moves. A standardised curriculum or core content that aligns across schools might also help minimise disruption for highly mobile learners.

2. *Enhance transition support*: We could develop more robust induction programmes for new learners to help them settle quickly. We might also appoint a Transition Mentor or similar role to provide guidance and support during school moves.

3. *Track and share data*: We could use digital systems to ensure that learner records, including progress data and individual support plans, are transferred seamlessly between schools. Local authorities could also collaborate to standardise data-sharing protocols.

4. *Provide emotional and pastoral support*: We could invest in well-being services such as counselling or peer mentoring, to help learners cope with the emotional challenges of mobility or parental deployment. For service children, we could also establish support groups where they can connect with peers in similar circumstances.

5. *Leverage the Service Pupil Premium (SPP)*: Schools receive additional funding for service children through the Service Pupil Premium. This funding should be used strategically to address specific needs, such as providing additional tuition, counselling, or extracurricular opportunities.

6. *Foster a sense of belonging:* We could foster a more inclusive school culture that welcomes new learners and celebrates diversity. We could also engage parents and families in school life to build stronger connections with families.

7. *Raise awareness among staff*: We might invest in training for teachers and staff to better understand the challenges faced by mobile learners and service children. And we might encourage staff to maintain high expectations for these learners and provide opportunities for them to excel.

8. *Support families*: We can work with local authorities and military organisations to offer resources and advice for families navigating frequent moves. Virtual support groups and networks for parents can also help them stay informed and involved in their children's education.

The attainment gap for service children and other highly mobile learners is a pressing issue, rooted in the instability and emotional challenges that come with frequent school moves. However, with the right interventions – such as improving transition processes, providing emotional and pastoral support, and leveraging resources like the Service Pupil Premium – we can help these children overcome barriers to success. By prioritising stability and inclusion, we can ensure that every child, regardless of their mobility, can thrive.

How the mobility gap intersects with inclusion and belonging

For service children and other learners experiencing high levels of mobility, a sense of inclusion and belonging plays a crucial role in their academic success. As we've seen, these children often face unique challenges due to frequent school moves, disrupted routines, and social isolation. Without a strong sense of connection to their school community, they are more likely to disengage, which exacerbates the attainment gap.

Children who move frequently often struggle to build lasting friendships, which can leave them feeling isolated. A lack of peer support can reduce their motivation to participate in school activities, both academically and socially. Belonging fosters the relationships needed for a supportive learning environment.

Frequent transitions can create a sense of instability, making it harder for children to feel grounded in their learning. A welcoming, inclusive school environment helps mitigate these feelings by offering consistent emotional and academic support. When schools actively include new learners, they help create a sense of permanence and safety, even if the child knows they may move again.

Mobile learners often experience a lack of continuity in relationships with teachers, which can hinder their ability to thrive. When teachers make a deliberate effort to build positive relationships and maintain high expectations, learners feel valued and included. For service children, understanding the unique pressures of parental deployment and offering empathy helps strengthen their sense of belonging.

Mobile learners, such as those from military families or Traveller communities, can feel out of place if their backgrounds are not recognised or respected. A lack of cultural awareness can lead to unconscious bias, stigmatisation, or exclusion. Creating a culture that celebrates diversity and values each child's experiences fosters belonging.

In practice, we might:

- Implement robust induction processes to help new learners settle in quickly. This might include assigning a buddy, giving tours, and offering tailored academic support during the transition period.

- Establish peer mentoring schemes or support groups for mobile learners – such as service children – to provide a space to share experiences and build connections with others in similar situations

- Adapt teaching methods to accommodate mobile learners, ensuring they can access the curriculum despite gaps in prior learning

- Encourage group work and collaborative projects to help foster friendships and inclusion in the classroom

- Incorporate lessons or activities that acknowledge and celebrate the backgrounds of service children and other mobile learners. For example, recognising Armed Forces Day or highlighting the contributions of Traveller communities can create a culture of respect and inclusion.

- Provide access to counselling or pastoral care for those service children who face emotional stress due to parental deployment

- Give all staff training to help them identify signs of emotional distress and intervene early

- Actively involve families in the school community, keeping them informed and encouraging their participation in events and activities

- Maintain strong communication during deployment periods to help parents stay connected to their children's education

Self-evaluation

Having read about the mobility gap, put the theory into practice by answering the following self-evaluative questions:

1. What are the primary challenges faced by service children and highly mobile learners in terms of their academic achievement?

2. How does frequent school mobility impact a child's ability to build relationships and maintain academic progress?

3. What role does emotional and social isolation play in the academic performance of mobile learners?

4. How has the attainment gap for service children evolved over the past 20 years, and what factors have influenced these changes?

5. What specific support strategies can schools implement to provide continuity of learning for highly mobile learners?

6. What is the Service Pupil Premium (SPP), and how can it be used effectively to support service children?

7. How can the emotional well-being of service children be better supported to help them overcome the challenges of parental deployment?

8. What are some practical ways that schools can foster a sense of inclusion and belonging for service children and other mobile learners?

9. How can teachers and staff be trained to better understand the unique challenges faced by service children and highly mobile learners?

10. In what ways can schools enhance their transition support for mobile learners to ensure that their academic and emotional needs are addressed?

10 Other causes of difference and disadvantage

Other than the characteristics I've already explored, what are the main causes of attainment gaps in school? Here are some other factors to consider . . .

1. Parental engagement and expectations

Parental involvement in their children's education can have a profound impact on attainment. Learners whose parents actively support their learning – through reading with them, helping with homework, or engaging with the school community – tend to achieve better outcomes. Conversely, learners from families with low levels of engagement or where there are language barriers may face additional challenges.

Parental expectations also matter. High expectations from parents, regardless of socio-economic background, are linked to better academic outcomes. When parents have lower expectations, learners may internalise these, affecting their motivation and aspirations.

2. School leadership and the quality of teaching

The quality of school leadership and teaching significantly affects learner outcomes. Schools with strong leadership that prioritise professional development, effective teaching strategies, and a culture of high expectations tend to perform better. In contrast, schools with less effective leadership and teaching may struggle to support all learners, particularly those from disadvantaged backgrounds.

Teacher quality is crucial for all learners, but particularly critical for disadvantaged and vulnerable learners. Research shows that effective teachers can significantly reduce attainment gaps by delivering tailored support and inspiring learners. In schools where teacher turnover is high or where teachers lack subject-specific training, learners are more likely to fall behind.

3. School resources and infrastructure

Access to resources – such as books, technology, extracurricular activities, and well-maintained school facilities – plays a role in determining learner achievement. Learners from schools with fewer resources are often at a disadvantage. The quality of school infrastructure, including access to safe play areas, libraries, and science labs, can also affect learning outcomes.

Funding disparities between schools can exacerbate attainment gaps. Underfunded schools may struggle to offer a full curriculum, employ specialist staff, or provide additional support services that benefit disadvantaged learners.

4. Teacher perception and bias

Unconscious bias among teachers can affect how they interact with learners from different backgrounds. This can influence learner assessment, classroom participation, and feedback. For instance, learners from minority ethnic backgrounds or those with low socio-economic status may receive less challenging work, less encouragement, or harsher disciplinary measures, which impacts their achievement.

Teacher perceptions of behaviour can also be influenced by factors such as socio-economic background or SEND, leading to different expectations and consequences. This can result in disproportionate exclusion rates or a lack of access to a broad curriculum.

5. Transition points

Transitions between key stages, such as moving from primary to secondary school or from secondary school to further education or employment, can be particularly challenging for some learners. Poor transitions often mean a lack of continuity in support, leading to gaps in learning and attainment.

6. Social and emotional well-being

Learners who face significant emotional or social challenges such as mental health issues, bullying, or family problems, are more likely to struggle academically. Schools that do not have adequate support systems in place may fail to address these underlying issues, leaving learners at risk of disengagement and underachievement.

Trauma and adverse childhood experiences (ACEs) can have long-term effects on academic performance, as they may interfere with concentration, behaviour, and motivation.

What can we do?

To address these wider causes of attainment gaps, we need to take a holistic approach which might involve:

1. *Strengthening parental involvement*

   - Actively engage parents as partners in their children's education, offering workshops, one-to-one meetings, and access to resources that support learning at home
   - Encourage parents to set high aspirations and provide positive reinforcement for academic and personal achievements

2. *Improving school leadership and teaching*

   - Ensure effective school leadership by focusing on continuous improvement, setting high standards, and providing adequate resources
   - Invest in professional development for teachers to build their expertise in diverse teaching methods and strategies that support all learners, including those from disadvantaged backgrounds

3. *Equitable resource allocation*

   - Allocate funding based on need, ensuring that all schools have the resources they require to deliver a high-quality education
   - Promote equity in access to technology, books, extracurricular activities, and specialist support

4. *Addressing bias and expectations*

   - Provide training for teachers on recognising and challenging their own biases. This could involve workshops, mentoring, or consultancy services.
   - Monitor tracking and disciplinary practices to ensure they are fair and do not disproportionately affect learners from certain backgrounds

5. *Supporting learners through transition*

   - Develop robust transition strategies that ensure learners move smoothly between phases of education. This includes ensuring continuity in support, maintaining regular communication with parents, and assessing and addressing any learning gaps.
   - Establish targeted interventions for learners who move schools frequently, such as bridging courses or catch-up classes

6. *Promoting social and emotional well-being*

   - Create a nurturing school environment where learners feel safe and valued. This can include access to counsellors, mental health resources, and peer support groups.

- Address barriers to learning by offering emotional support and practical help for learners dealing with challenging personal circumstances

Attainment gaps are complex and multi-faceted, extending beyond demographic factors to include school culture, resources, teacher quality, and learner well-being. To close these gaps, we need to adopt a systemic approach that addresses the root causes, ensures all learners feel included and valued, and provides tailored support where it is most needed.

Creating an inclusive school

Inclusion aims to integrate learners with additional needs into mainstream classrooms while fostering an environment that benefits all learners. For learners with disabilities, inclusion offers significant opportunities for growth. They gain chances to build friendships, develop communication skills, and enhance their independence across various areas of functioning. Being part of a mainstream environment contributes to their self-esteem and self-efficacy, while access to the same curriculum as their peers exposes them to higher academic standards and social expectations. This prepares them for adulthood in a more inclusive society. Additionally, peer interactions provide models of appropriate behaviour and social skills that learners with disabilities can emulate.

Other learners also gain from inclusive settings. They learn to appreciate individual differences, fostering a culture of respect and understanding. Exposure to peers with disabilities broadens their awareness of diversity and challenges stereotypes about what individuals with disabilities can achieve.

Inclusive settings also encourage the development of interpersonal skills, such as helping others and working collaboratively.

Inclusion can transform schools. Collaborative practices among staff increase, leading to the sharing of expertise and the adoption of evidence-based teaching methods. Communication with parents deepens, too, and connections with external services strengthen. This helps create a supportive community in which the needs of all learners are met more effectively.

Successful inclusion requires careful planning and a school-wide commitment. Leadership from senior leaders sets the tone, fostering a culture that values every learner. A whole-school approach ensures that inclusion becomes part of the ethos, with all teachers contributing positively. Policies need to clearly outline roles and responsibilities, providing a framework that supports collaboration among teachers and support staff.

Time is a crucial resource. Teachers require opportunities to plan, communicate, and evaluate their strategies regularly. Continuous professional development equips educators with adaptive teaching techniques and skills for differentiating instruction. Engaging parents as partners in their children's education is equally important, as their insights and support can significantly enhance outcomes.

While the benefits of inclusion are clear, challenges persist. Large class sizes, inadequate funding, and insufficient access to resources can hinder progress. Schools can address these issues by prioritising flexible groupings and investing in assistive technologies.

Collaboration with external services ensures that specialised support, such as speech therapy or psychological assessments, is available when needed. Negative attitudes among staff or learners require targeted training and awareness programmes to promote acceptance and understanding. Physical barriers should also be addressed to guarantee accessibility for learners with mobility challenges.

In today's classrooms, diversity extends across cultural, socioeconomic, and ability spectrums. Teachers must adapt to meet the varying needs of their learners. Effective differentiation involves adjusting teaching methods, curriculum content, and classroom resources. For instance, lessons can be designed to build on learners' prior knowledge while incorporating scaffolding techniques to help those who may need extra support.

High expectations are essential for all learners. For example, girls' self-efficacy in maths and science can be bolstered through inclusive teaching strategies that counteract traditional stereotypes. Similarly, children from disadvantaged backgrounds benefit from a curriculum that exposes them to new experiences and encourages them to aim high. In multicultural classrooms, culturally responsive teaching recognises and values the unique contributions of all learners, fostering an inclusive environment where everyone feels that they belong.

Effective teaching in inclusive classrooms requires thoughtful planning and delivery. Direct teaching methods – teacher explanations and modelling – can be especially valuable when introducing learners to new topics or when clarifying complex concepts. Breaking content into manageable steps, using repetition, and providing ongoing feedback also help to reinforce learning for all learners. Interactive teaching methods, such as class discussions and questioning, keep learners engaged and provide many opportunities to assess their understanding.

Teachers should also utilise a variety of resources to support diverse learners. Visual aids, simplified texts, and assistive technologies, such as screen readers or voice recognition software, make content more accessible. For example, using decodable books for early readers or providing captioned videos for learners with hearing impairments ensures that everyone can engage with the material.

Assessment is a critical component of inclusive education. It not only measures learner progress but also informs teaching strategies. Observing learners during tasks, engaging them in oral questioning, and reviewing their portfolios provide valuable insights into their understanding and needs. Regular assessments enable teachers to identify when learners require additional support or enrichment.

Tests and assignments should be designed with inclusivity in mind. Providing clear instructions, offering varied question types, and allowing alternative formats for responses ensures that all learners can demonstrate their knowledge effectively. For example, a learner with dyslexia might present their work orally or through a digital medium. Grading should reflect both effort and achievement, with constructive feedback guiding further improvement.

Some practical take-aways

Inclusion doesn't happen by accident. Schools need to consider these critical enablers:

- Leadership: A leadership team's commitment shapes a supportive culture.
- Whole-school approach: Positive attitudes and collaborative policies drive inclusion.
- Teacher skills: Staff require adaptive teaching methods and teamwork.
- Support systems: Regular communication with support staff and specialists ensures consistency.
- Planning time: Teachers need opportunities to prepare and evaluate strategies.
- Parental involvement: Families play an integral role in the learner's journey.

Inclusion has its obstacles, but these can be mitigated:

- Class sizes: Flexible groupings and technology can alleviate strain.
- Resources: Schools should advocate for funding and access external services.
- Negative attitudes: Staff training and learner-led initiatives promote acceptance.
- Physical barriers: Accessibility adaptations ensure mobility for all learners.

Learners bring varied backgrounds, experiences, and abilities to the classroom. Teachers can adapt by:

- Differentiating instruction: Tailoring lessons to accommodate varying needs
- Ensuring high expectations: Challenging stereotypes, especially around gender and socioeconomic backgrounds
- Being culturally responsive: Leveraging learners' cultural capital while promoting mutual respect

Instructional adaptations include:

- Breaking it down: Presenting material in manageable steps, or 'chunks'
- Interactive teaching: Engaging learners actively with questions and discussions
- Repetition and feedback: Reinforcing learning with clear and constructive input

Resource adjustments include:

- Visual aids: Pictures, diagrams, and videos to enhance understanding
- Simplified text: Modifying reading material for clarity and accessibility
- Assistive technology: Tools like screen readers or speech-to-text apps which empower learners

Assessment strategies include:

- Variety in tasks: Using multiple question types and formats to assess understanding
- Effort and achievement: Providing separate grades to recognise persistence and mastery
- Personalised support: Adapting test settings and formats to learner needs

Self-evaluation

Having read about other causes of attainment gaps, put the theory into practice by answering the following self-evaluative questions:

1. How can you actively encourage and support parental involvement in your students' education to help close the attainment gap?
2. What steps can you take within your role to contribute to strong leadership and promote a culture of high expectations in your school?
3. In what ways can you advocate for or contribute to ensuring equitable access to resources for all learners in your school?
4. How can you reflect on and challenge any potential unconscious biases you may hold when interacting with learners from different backgrounds?
5. What strategies can you use to help students navigate transitions between key stages to reduce the potential for attainment gaps?
6. How can you support the emotional and social well-being of students who may face challenges outside of school?
7. How can you create a more inclusive classroom that accommodates the diverse needs of learners, particularly those with disabilities or from disadvantaged backgrounds?
8. What specific adaptations can you make to your teaching methods to support the varied learning needs in your classroom?

9. How can you better engage with parents to ensure they feel supported in helping their children achieve academically?

10. How can you adapt your assessment strategies to be more inclusive and reflective of each learner's unique strengths and challenges?

***

I said I'd return to what this looked like in practice and explore in greater depth features of inclusive lesson planning, teaching, and assessment. So, let's do just that. We'll start with lesson planning . . .

PART THREE
Inclusive planning, teaching, and assessment

11 Inclusive lesson planning

Inclusive lesson planning requires 3Cs:

1. Cross-curricular connections

2. Classroom consistency

3. Connections to the real world

Let's explore each feature in turn . . .

1. Cross-curricular connections

We can support disadvantaged learners to succeed at school by helping them to make more sense of the school curriculum. The more meaning we can attach to the curriculum, making abstract information more concrete and real, connecting the new with the familiar, the more able learners will be to transfer that knowledge across domains. A part of this is finding connections across the school curriculum, enabling subject disciplines to talk to each other and complement each other.

Finding natural connections between subject disciplines across the school curriculum helps promote deeper understanding. By linking subjects, learners can see how knowledge in one area complements and enhances another. For instance, studying statistics in maths alongside climate data in geography helps learners grasp both the practical application of mathematical concepts and the real-world implications of environmental change. These connections move learners beyond surface-level understanding to a more integrated grasp of the material.

Making connections also boosts active participation because when learners recognise the relevance of what they're studying they're likely to be more engaged in it. For example, an English lesson exploring persuasive writing could tie into history by analysing famous speeches from key historical figures. This approach makes learning feel purposeful, demonstrating how skills are transferable across disciplines and into life beyond school.

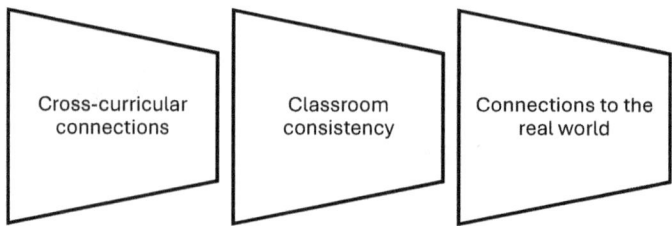

Figure 11.1 3Cs of lesson planning

Drawing cross-curricular links also helps foster critical thinking because such connections encourage learners to synthesise information from multiple sources. For example, combining science and art to study the anatomy of the human body nurtures analytical and creative thinking. This dual perspective helps learners approach problems in innovative ways, preparing them for complex, real-world challenges.

When subjects are interlinked, learners naturally practise a range of skills simultaneously. A project on designing an eco-friendly building, for instance, might incorporate science (energy efficiency), maths (measurements and budgets), and design technology (architecture). Such activities mirror workplace scenarios where interdisciplinary skills are crucial.

Teachers collaborating across departments model teamwork for their learners. Interdisciplinary projects often require learners to work together, bringing diverse perspectives to a shared goal. This collaborative spirit builds social skills, resilience, and adaptability – key attributes for both academic and future career success.

A connected curriculum helps avoid the fragmentation that can sometimes occur in siloed subject teaching. For example, themes like sustainability or human rights can underpin lessons across multiple subjects, creating a coherent narrative that reinforces learning. Learners are less likely to view their education as a series of isolated topics and more as a unified journey.

Life rarely presents problems neatly categorised into 'maths', 'science', or 'history'. Cross-disciplinary teaching mimics the complexity of real-world challenges, equipping learners with the tools to approach them holistically. Whether they're analysing data, solving logistical problems, or creating persuasive presentations, learners benefit from integrated thinking.

A word of warning, though: To achieve these benefits, we should look for natural overlaps between subjects rather than forcing connections. We should also start small and introduce shared terminology, coordinate assessment themes, or plan joint projects with colleagues. Gradually, these efforts can lead to a more cohesive curriculum that supports learners' academic and personal development.

It's worth noting that integrating disciplines doesn't dilute the rigour of individual subjects; it enhances it. By demonstrating how knowledge and skills interconnect, we can inspire a generation of learners who are curious, capable, and ready to tackle the challenges of an interconnected world.

Here are some examples of cross-curricular links:

Theme 1: Sustainability

- Geography: Explore climate change, renewable energy sources, and sustainable urban planning
- Science: Investigate the chemistry of greenhouse gases and renewable energy technologies such as solar panels
- Design technology: Design eco-friendly products or prototypes for sustainable housing
- Maths: Analyse statistical data on global carbon emissions or calculate energy savings from green initiatives
- English: Write persuasive essays or speeches advocating for environmental action

Theme 2: Identity and culture

- History: Study the evolution of cultural identities, such as the impact of immigration on British society
- Art: Create visual representations of cultural heritage, using symbolism to explore identity
- English: Analyse literature or poetry that reflects themes of belonging and self-discovery
- Modern foreign languages: Learn about traditions, festivals, and social norms in French-, German-, or Spanish-speaking countries
- Music: Explore cultural influences in musical styles and compositions from around the world

Theme 3: Innovation and technology

- Computing: Develop coding skills to create apps or programmes addressing real-world challenges
- Science: Study the physics behind technological advancements like robotics or artificial intelligence
- Design technology: Design and build prototypes for innovative gadgets or machines
- Business studies: Create business plans for marketing the technology learners have designed
- Maths: Model financial predictions or optimise designs using mathematical concepts

Theme 4: Human Rights

- History: Investigate pivotal moments in human rights movements, such as the abolition of slavery or the suffragette movement
- Religious studies: Discuss moral and ethical perspectives on human rights across different faiths
- English: Examine speeches, such as Martin Luther King Jr.'s *I Have a Dream*, to explore rhetorical techniques
- Drama: Recreate historical moments or perform plays that address social justice issues
- PSHE: Reflect on contemporary human rights issues, including equality and inclusion

Theme 5: Health and well-being

- Physical education: Teach the importance of regular exercise and its impact on physical and mental health
- Science: Explore the biology of the human body, such as the cardiovascular system or the effects of nutrition on health
- Food technology: Develop healthy recipes and understand the nutritional science behind meal planning
- PSHE: Address mental health awareness, resilience, and mindfulness practices
- Maths: Analyse data on health trends, such as obesity rates or the effectiveness of fitness programmes

Theme 6: Space exploration

- Science: Study the physics of space travel and the chemistry of rocket fuel
- Maths: Calculate trajectories and distances between planets
- Geography: Discuss the impact of satellite technology on mapping and weather prediction
- Art: Create visual interpretations of space, such as abstract depictions of galaxies or astronauts
- English: Write science fiction stories or debate the ethics of space colonisation

Of course, planning such connections can be time-consuming and logistically challenging. To help the process, teachers should meet regularly to identify opportunities for collaboration and ensure coherence across subjects – and this meeting time needs to form part of a teacher's contracted hours, not be left to their goodwill.

Joint activities, such as a cross-subject week or shared assessment tasks, are often a manageable – smaller scale – way to begin. And we could encourage learners to take some ownership by working on interdisciplinary projects, such as creating presentations, portfolios, or displays that draw on multiple disciplines.

Making cross-curricular connections is one way to ensure more inclusive lesson planning. But it's by no means the only way . . .

2. Classroom consistency

Classroom consistency is also key to curriculum success. The more consistency there is in what we teach and how we teach it, the more able learners will be to access the curriculum and understand it. Consistency across subject disciplines – especially when teaching shared concepts or methods like mathematical techniques or essay-writing – offers significant advantages for learners and teachers alike. By aligning approaches, we provide clarity, reduce cognitive load, and ensure that learning is transferable.

Here's why consistency matters:

Consistency reduces confusion for learners

When different subjects approach the same concept in varied or conflicting ways, learners can become confused. For example, if one subject uses a specific method for structuring essays and another deviates, learners may struggle to know what is expected. Consistency creates a clear roadmap for learners, helping them focus on mastering skills rather than deciphering varying approaches to instruction. By way of illustration, a standardised essay structure, such as Point-Evidence-Explain (PEE), could be used across English, history, and geography. This reinforces the process and allows learners to focus on content rather than format.

Consistency builds confidence and competence

Repeating consistent methods across disciplines helps learners internalise key concepts. This familiarity breeds confidence, as they know how to tackle tasks regardless of the subject. It also strengthens competence by giving them more opportunities to practise and refine their skills. For example, mathematical methods, like solving equations or interpreting graphs, should be taught using the same terminology and processes in maths, science, and geography. This ensures learners can apply their knowledge seamlessly in different contexts.

Consistency encourages the development of transferable skills

Consistency helps learners see how skills and knowledge connect across subjects. This reinforces the idea that what they learn in one area has value elsewhere, promoting a holistic approach to education and preparing them for real-world problem-solving. For example, a persuasive writing technique taught in English can be used in history to construct an argument about a historical event or in

PSHE to advocate for a cause. Consistent terminology and expectations make this transfer easier.

Consistency improves efficiency in learning

When methods are consistent, teachers don't need to re-teach the basics for each subject. Instead, they can focus on subject-specific content, allowing learners to progress more quickly and deeply in their learning. For example, teaching learners a universal method for analysing texts – such as identifying audience, purpose, and techniques (APT) – means they can apply this framework in English, religious education, or even art analysis without needing a separate explanation.

Consistency supports adaptive teaching and inclusion

A consistent approach can be particularly beneficial for learners who require additional support, such as those with special educational needs. Familiarity reduces anxiety and cognitive load, helping all learners access the curriculum more equitably. For example, using a standard method for breaking down complex tasks – like annotating texts or tackling multi-step maths problems – ensures every learner has a reliable starting point.

Consistency enhances teacher collaboration

Consistency fosters better collaboration among teachers. When staff agree on shared methods and concepts, they can build on one another's work rather than duplicating effort. It also enables better communication about learners' progress and areas for improvement. For example, a school-wide agreement on how to teach graph interpretation means science and maths teachers can plan lessons that complement each other, reinforcing learner understanding.

Consistency helps prepare learners for assessments

Exams often require learners to apply the same skills across different subjects. Consistency in teaching ensures they are well-prepared, knowing what is expected and how to deliver it effectively. For example, standardising essay-writing approaches across English, history, and geography aligns well with GCSE and A Level expectations, where coherent arguments and structured writing are key.

To implement this strategy, it's wise to start by establishing shared methods, such as a universal essay structure or graph-analysis technique. Then, ensure all subjects use the same language to describe key skills, like 'hypothesis' or 'evaluation'. Next, offer professional development sessions to align teaching strategies across disciplines. And develop templates or guides that can be adapted for each subject, ensuring consistency without losing subject specificity.

By ensuring consistency across disciplines, schools can create a more cohesive and supportive learning environment. As a result, learners gain confidence, competence, and clarity, while teachers work more effectively together.

3. Connections to the real world

Earlier, I argued that we should make connections between subject disciplines. But that's not all. We should also connect what we teach with the world beyond our school gates because using real-world examples in teaching is a powerful tool for making learning more relevant, engaging, and impactful. For disadvantaged learners, who may have fewer opportunities to experience certain cultural, social, or professional contexts, these examples also play a critical role in building cultural capital.

Here's why making real-world connections matters:

Real-world examples help learners connect abstract concepts to their own lives and experiences. For disadvantaged learners, this relevance can demystify unfamiliar ideas and make the curriculum feel accessible rather than remote or academic. For example, teaching percentages by comparing supermarket discounts or interest rates on loans shows how maths applies to everyday decisions, giving learners practical tools for managing their future finances.

Many disadvantaged learners may not have access to the same breadth of experiences – such as museums, professional networks, or travel – that their peers take for granted. By incorporating real-world examples, we can provide insights into these worlds, enriching learners' understanding of society and its opportunities. For example, a history lesson on the Industrial Revolution could include a discussion about how modern engineering careers evolved, alongside visits to local heritage sites or virtual tours of factories.

When learners see the relevance of what they're learning, they're more likely to stay engaged. Real-world examples can spark curiosity and inspire ambition by showing how the curriculum connects to jobs, hobbies, and global issues. For example, linking English lessons on persuasive writing to creating marketing campaigns or writing for social media gives learners a tangible reason to master these skills.

Disadvantaged learners may have limited exposure to role models in certain professions or cultural activities. Using examples from diverse fields, such as medicine, law, or the arts, broadens their horizons and helps them see a place for themselves in these areas. For example, in science, lessons on biology could feature case studies of doctors or researchers from similar backgrounds to the learners, highlighting potential career paths.

Real-world examples encourage learners to think critically about the world around them, preparing them for adult life. For disadvantaged learners, who may have fewer opportunities to develop these skills at home, this is particularly vital. For example, in geography, teaching about urban planning through discussions of local housing developments or transport systems fosters problem-solving skills and an awareness of civic responsibilities.

By integrating examples from literature, art, or history that reflect diverse perspectives and global cultures, we can build learners' cultural literacy. This enriches their understanding of the world and equips them to participate in broader societal conversations. For example, a study of Shakespeare's *Othello* could include discussions of race and identity, helping learners understand historical and contemporary issues while building empathy.

Cultural capital is a key driver of social justice. By exposing learners to real-world examples – whether through case studies, guest speakers, or trips – we can help to level the playing field, giving disadvantaged learners insights and experiences that prepare them for higher education and employment. For example, a project in business studies might involve a visit to a local company or a virtual Q&A with entrepreneurs, showing learners what it takes to succeed in business.

Real-world examples make education feel like a continuous journey rather than a series of disconnected lessons. For disadvantaged learners, this approach can nurture curiosity and encourage them to see learning as integral to their personal and professional growth. For example, linking environmental science lessons to community recycling initiatives or climate action projects demonstrates how learners can make a difference in their own lives.

To make real-world connections, it's helpful to start with examples that resonate with learners' everyday experiences before introducing unfamiliar ideas. Then, use virtual tours, online case studies, and digital resources to provide access to experiences that might otherwise be out of reach. Next, bring in local businesses, charities, or cultural organisations to provide real-world contexts for learning. And finally, show how real-world issues connect across subjects, such as using climate change as a theme in geography, science, and PSHE.

By embedding real-world examples into teaching, we can inspire disadvantaged learners, build their cultural capital, and equip them with the knowledge and skills to navigate and shape the world around them. This not only enriches their education but also empowers them to aspire, achieve, and thrive.

Self-evaluation

Having read about inclusive lesson planning, put the theory into practice by answering the following self-evaluative questions:

1. How effectively do I currently identify and leverage natural connections between subject disciplines in my lesson planning?

2. What are some examples of interdisciplinary projects I could introduce to foster deeper understanding and engagement in my classroom?

3. How do I ensure that cross-curricular links are authentic and not forced, providing genuine value to learners' learning experiences?

4. Do I collaborate with colleagues across departments to align teaching methods and shared concepts, such as essay structures or graph interpretation?

5. What steps could I take to ensure consistency in terminology and methods across subjects in my school?

6. How do I currently support learners in transferring skills learned in one subject to other disciplines or real-world applications?

7. How often do I incorporate real-world examples into my lessons, and how relevant are they to my learners' lives and experiences?

8. In what ways can I better use real-world connections to build my learners' cultural capital, particularly for disadvantaged learners?

9. What opportunities exist in my local community (e.g. businesses, cultural organisations, guest speakers) that I could tap into in order to enhance real-world relevance in my teaching?

10. Which of the three pillars – cross-curricular connections, cross-curricular consistency, or real-world connections – is most underdeveloped in my current teaching practice, and why?

12 Inclusive teaching

Whilst the whole of this book explores inclusive classroom practices, this chapter looks specifically at ways of ensuring that every child can access the same ambitious curriculum and achieve their potential. We will examine the difference between traditional differentiation and adaptive or responsive teaching and explore some practical examples of using task-scaffolding to make learning accessible to all.

The first point to note is that adaptive or responsive teaching is not an add-on or afterthought; rather, it is integral to quality first teaching. Quality first teaching takes place when the teacher designs an ambitious, broad and balanced, and planned and sequenced curriculum and teaches that curriculum to every learner – thus achieving equality – but then ensures that ever learner can indeed access that curriculum and attain – thus achieving equity.

Adaptive teaching is also front and centre in the Teachers' Standards and the Initial Teacher Training and Early Career Framework (ITTECF) . . .

According to Standard 5 of the Teachers' Standards (DfE, 2011)[1] adaptive teaching is when teachers "adapt teaching to respond to the strengths and needs of all pupils". Specifically, adaptive teaching requires teachers to:

- Know when and how to differentiate appropriately, using approaches which enable pupils to be taught effectively

- Have a secure understanding of how a range of factors can inhibit pupils' ability to learn and how best to overcome these

- Demonstrate an awareness of the physical, social, and intellectual development of children and know how to adapt teaching to support pupils' education at different stages of development

- Have a clear understanding of the needs of all pupils – including those with SEND, those of high ability, those with English as an additional language – and be able to use and evaluate distinctive teaching approaches to engage and support them

As I say, adaptive teaching also forms part of the Initial Teacher Training and Early Career Framework (DfE, 2024).[2] Section 5 of the ECF says that new teachers should learn that:

- Pupils are likely to learn at different rates and to require different levels and types of support from teachers to succeed.
- Seeking to understand pupils' differences, including their different levels of prior knowledge and potential barriers to learning, is an essential part of teaching.
- Adapting teaching in a responsive way, including by providing targeted support to pupils who are struggling, is likely to increase pupil success.
- Adaptive teaching is less likely to be valuable if it causes the teacher to artificially create distinct tasks for different groups of pupils or to set lower expectations for particular pupils.
- Flexibly grouping pupils within a class to provide more tailored support can be effective, but care should be taken to monitor the impact on engagement and motivation, particularly for low attaining pupils.
- There is a common misconception that pupils have distinct and identifiable learning styles. This is not supported by evidence and attempting to tailor lessons to learning styles is unlikely to be beneficial.
- Pupils with SEND are likely to require additional or adapted support, working closely with colleagues, families, and pupils to understand barriers and identify effective strategies is essential.

According to the ECF, new teachers also need to learn how to:

- Develop an understanding of different pupil needs, including by identifying pupils who need new content further broken down, using formative assessment and working closely with the SENCO and others
- Provide opportunity for all pupils to experience success, including by maintaining high expectations for all and making effective use of teaching assistants
- Meet individual needs without creating unnecessary workload, including by planning to connect new content with pupils' existing knowledge or providing additional pre-teaching; building in additional practice; reframing questions to provide greater scaffolding; and "considering carefully whether intervening within lessons with individuals and small groups would be more efficient and effective than planning different lessons for different groups of pupils"
- Group pupils effectively, including by applying high expectations to all groups, changing groups regularly, and ensuring that any groups based on attainment are subject specific

In sum, whereas traditional differentiation focuses on individual learners or small groups of learners, adaptive teaching focuses on the whole class. It is the difference between teaching up to 30 different lessons at once, matching the pace and pitch to each learner and providing different tasks and resources to different learners, and teaching the same lesson to all 30 learners, by 'teaching to the top' and providing scaffolds to those who need additional initial support.

Crucially, additional support offered in the guise of scaffolding should be reduced over time so that all learners can become increasingly independent.

The problem with the former approach – teaching up to 30 different lessons – is that, as well as it being hugely time-consuming for the teacher, it can translate in practice as expecting less of some learners than we do of others – in other words, as dumbing down or reducing the curriculum on offer.

Unlike traditional forms of differentiation which can perpetuate attainment gaps by capping opportunities and aspirations, adaptive teaching promotes high achievement for all.

Put simply, if we dumb down or reduce the curriculum for some learners, we only serve to double their existing differences and disadvantages, rather than help them overcome those challenges to achieve in line with their peers.

But what does this look like in practice?

Differentiation is marked by:

- Different curricula
- Different tasks
- Different expectations
- Different feedback
- Different levels of challenge
- Different outcomes

Whereas adaptive teaching is marked by:

- The same ambitious curriculum
- The same tasks
- The same high expectations
- The same demanding feedback
- The same level of challenge
- Scaffolds to make this accessible

These 'scaffolds' – like the scaffolding on a building – are temporary support structures that enable learners to reach higher levels of challenge. They are short-term

Inclusive teaching

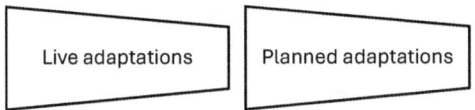

Figure 12.1 Live and planned adaptations

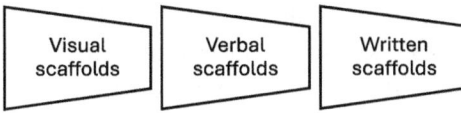

Figure 12.2 Visual, verbal, and written scaffolds

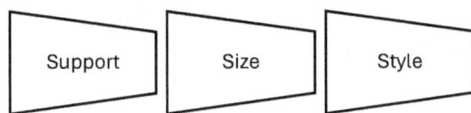

Figure 12.3 Types of adaptation: Support, size, and style

alterations that are made to the way we teach the curriculum – extra or different things – in order to allow all learners to access that curriculum.

Those alterations might be *live adaptations* which are 'in the moment' tweaks made in response to ongoing formative assessment and/or learner observation (such as a repeated or chunked instruction). Or they might be *planned adaptations* which are regular additional support given to those learners with known needs (such as the use of a teaching assistant, tailored worksheets, etc). Planned adaptations might also be the reasonable adjustments we make for learners with SEND to ensure we do not discriminate against those with protected characteristics as defined under the Equality Act 2010.

Task scaffolds might be *visual* – such as giving a learner a task planner, a list of small steps to take to complete a task, worked examples, images that support vocabulary learning, and so on.

Task scaffolds might be *verbal* – such as explaining a task in more explicit terms and in smaller steps, repeating an instruction, reteaching a difficult concept, using questioning to address misconceptions, and so on.

And task scaffolds might be *written* – such as a word bank, a writing frame, sentence starters, and so on.

Visual, verbal, and written task scaffolds are forms of additional or different types of support we can offer learners to help them get started with the same task as their peers. But we can also vary the size and style of a learner's finished product in order to ensure equity. For example, we might allow some learners to produce a shorter piece of work initially, or to plan out in brief rather than write their response in full. Crucially, they complete the same task as the rest of the class, but the volume of work expected of some learners is adjusted to match their current performance or needs.

Likewise, we might adjust the style of their work, giving some learners free reign whilst others are given a structure to follow or a set of signposts to use, perhaps even topic sentences at the start of every paragraph.

How to know what adjustments to make

Knowing whether to make these adjustments and when to make – and scale back or remove – these adjustments is key to the success of adaptive teaching. And there is no hard and fast rule to obey; rather, it's a case of trial and error in response to ongoing low-stakes formative assessments.

But there are some considerations to make.

Challenge is determined by the things a learner already knows. If a learner knows an area of study well, then the same question on the same content will be less challenging to them than it will to a learner whose prior knowledge is limited. The four challenge variables are therefore:

1. The intrinsic demand of the task: In other words, how difficult the task is in itself and how much it will stretch learners

2. Cognitive load: How much a learner will have to think about at once in order to understand and complete the task. The more a learner has to think about, the harder it will be to complete the task.

3. Prior knowledge: How much a learner already knows on the subject of the task. The more a learner knows about the subject of the task, the easier they will find it.

4. External support: How much additional support is provided to help with memory demands. This might include help from the teacher or a teaching assistant, or indeed from other learners.

Being aware of these four variables helps us to make appropriate adjustments. We can increase or decrease the challenge of a task – without changing the task itself – by:

1. *Sequencing* learning to make the bigger picture explicit

2. *Adapting* and chunking the number of things a learner has to think about

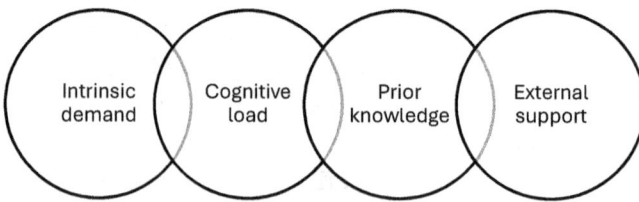

Figure 12.4 Four challenge variables

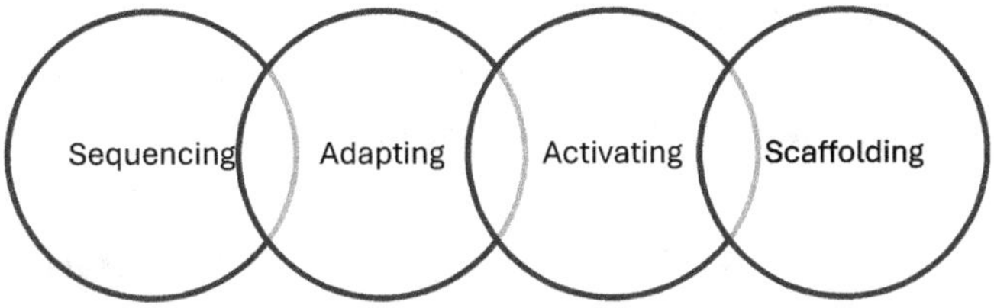

Inclusive teaching

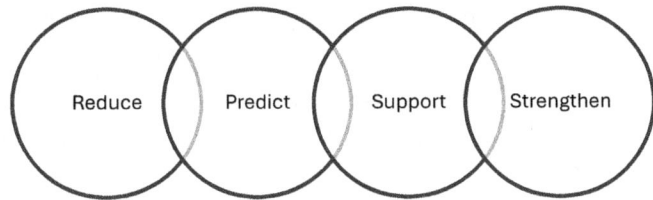

Figure 12.5 Four ways of adapting the challenge of a task

Figure 12.6 Four tips for making a success of adaptations

3. *Activating* prior knowledge through retrieval practice immediately before the task is begun

4. *Scaffolding* for memory demands

It might be helpful to think of this like a mixing desk whereby you slide four controls up or down depending on the challenge required.

Here are my top four tips for making sure our mixing desk produces melodic results:

REDUCE cognitive load – chunk and check

This is about breaking curriculum content or task instructions into smaller steps and checking a learner's understanding of each step before moving on to the next step.

PREDICT cognitive load – sequence, repeat, reinforce

This is about anticipating memory demands by sequencing the curriculum into a logical order so that key information is front-loaded, in other words key knowledge or skills are taught before they are needed in practice. It's also about connecting the curriculum, making meaning by making the links between various aspects of subject knowledge explicit. In short, it's about preparing learners for tasks by digging the foundations needed, and deepening learners' understanding of curriculum content by making it concrete and contextual.

SUPPORT cognitive load – scaffold and hold

This is about holding back some memory demands by providing additional or different types of support to learners so that they can think about the same content as everyone else in the class. The information held back is then introduced in small stages, thus ensuring those learners being supported through scaffolds do not develop learned helplessness but rather become increasingly independent.

STRENGTHEN cognitive load – retrieve and apply

This is about embedding frequent retrieval practice into the curriculum – indeed, into every lesson – so that prior knowledge is repeatedly activated in order to prevent knowledge decay, and so that it remains accessible to learners as they begin a task.

Here are some examples of adaptive teaching in practice . . .

In English, when teaching a complex novel such as *Wuthering Heights* we might give learners a simplified summary of the plot and some pen portraits of the key characters, as well as a family tree, before reading the text. We might also give learners a list of unfamiliar words – such as dialect – used in the novel, along with definitions.

When asking learners to write an essay about the novel later, we might first model how to structure the essay and we might write the essay's introduction on the board, thinking aloud as we do so. Next, learners might work in pairs to write their own introductions before writing the remainder of the essay individually. We might adapt this task further for those who would struggle to work independently by providing them with a writing frame for the essay or a set of topic sentences to begin each paragraph.

In maths, when teaching long division, we might break down the process into smaller steps, then model each step and get learners to practise in pairs before completing some questions independently. Learners requiring more support might be given scaffolded questions to complete, perhaps with partially completed answers, whilst others are given more challenging questions which contain real-world applications.

In history, when teaching World War Two, we might provide a blank timeline for learners to fill in as they learn about key events but, for some learners in need of additional support, we might offer a partially completed timeline instead, leaving only a few gaps for them to complete themselves.

In PE, when teaching football, we might divide learners into groups based on their current skills level. Inexperienced players might practise dribbling the ball and different passing techniques, with some explicit modelling, whilst more experienced players play a match that allows for the development of more advanced skills such as different formations and forcing the off-side trap. Such a strategy will allow inexperienced players to receive more direct feedback, whilst experienced players are encouraged to reflect on their own performance.

Self-evaluation

Having read about inclusive teaching, put the theory into practice by answering the following self-evaluative questions:

1. What are the key differences between traditional differentiation and adaptive teaching, and why is the latter considered more equitable?
2. How do I ensure that my lessons reflect the principles of 'teaching to the top' while providing the necessary scaffolds to support all learners?
3. Can I identify examples of visual, verbal, and written scaffolds that I currently use or could incorporate into my future teaching?
4. How do I monitor and plan to reduce scaffolding over time to encourage learner independence?
5. How effectively do I use low-stakes formative assessments to inform live and planned adaptations for individual learners?
6. Do I have strategies in place to address the needs of learners with SEND, EAL learners, and high-ability learners without creating distinct tasks or lowering expectations?
7. How do I ensure that I'm not relying on unsupported practices, such as tailoring lessons to presumed learning styles, in my teaching?
8. Am I thoughtfully grouping learners in ways that maximise learning opportunities without negatively affecting engagement or motivation?
9. How do I balance the four challenge variables (intrinsic demand, cognitive load, prior knowledge, and external support) when designing tasks to meet diverse needs?
10. What steps can I take to continuously improve my ability to adapt teaching strategies responsively and equitably while maintaining high expectations for all learners?

Notes

1 https://www.gov.uk/government/publications/teachers-standards
2 https://www.gov.uk/government/publications/initial-teacher-training-and-early-career-framework

13 Inclusive assessment

School assessments are a vital part of education, measuring progress and guiding learning. However, they can unintentionally discriminate against certain groups of learners, creating barriers to fair outcomes. By acknowledging and better understanding these issues, we can develop more inclusive practices, ensuring that all learners have an equal opportunity to succeed.

Assessments can be discriminatory in the following ways:

Cultural capital bias

Assessments often reflect the experiences, language, and values of the dominant culture, disadvantaging learners from diverse cultural backgrounds. For instance, exam questions or reading materials may assume familiarity with specific customs, idioms, or historical events that not all learners share.

For example, a comprehension exercise referencing activities like skiing holidays may alienate learners from less affluent or urban backgrounds.

Language barriers

Learners for whom English is an additional language may struggle with assessments that prioritise language proficiency over subject knowledge. This places them at a disadvantage, even when they understand the underlying concepts.

For example, a science exam that requires detailed written explanations rather than diagrams or practical demonstrations may disadvantage EAL learners.

Socio-economic disparities

Learners from disadvantaged backgrounds may lack access to resources that support assessment preparation, such as private tutoring, internet access, or quiet study spaces. This can affect their ability to perform well compared to peers with greater access to these advantages.

For example, homework-based assessments can disadvantage learners who don't have access to a computer or a supportive home environment.

Special educational needs and disabilities (SEND)

Traditional assessments often fail to accommodate the needs of SEND learners. Time-limited exams or a reliance on written assessments, for instance, don't always allow for an accurate reflection of the abilities of learners with dyslexia, ADHD, or processing difficulties. Further, a timed maths test requiring quick mental calculations might not fairly assess a learner with dyscalculia.

Gender stereotypes

Assessment design can inadvertently reinforce gender stereotypes, leading to different outcomes for boys and girls. For instance, questions or topics perceived as 'masculine' or 'feminine' might engage one gender more than the other.

Take, for example, a physics exam question framed around engineering contexts – which may inadvertently favour boys if girls have had less exposure to these concepts due to societal biases.

Over-emphasis on one type of intelligence

Traditional assessments often prioritise academic intelligence, such as logical reasoning or linguistic skills, at the expense of other abilities like creativity, practical skills, or interpersonal intelligence. This can disadvantage learners with strengths in non-academic areas.

For example, an art project assessed solely on written analysis of techniques may undervalue practical artistic ability.

So, what can we do about it?

We can make assessment more inclusive by:

Diversifying assessment formats: We could use a range of assessment methods to accommodate different learning styles and strengths. For instance, we could combine written exams with oral presentations, practical demonstrations, and group projects. For example, in science we could assess learners on their ability to conduct experiments, interpret data, and explain findings verbally, not just through written exams.

Providing adjustments for SEND learners: We could ensure assessments are designed with SEND learners in mind. This might include offering extra time, alternative formats (e.g. audio or visual), or the use of assistive technology. Collaboration with SEND coordinators is essential here. For example, a dyslexic learner might complete a history exam using voice-to-text software rather than writing by hand.

Ensuring cultural relevance: We could create assessment materials that reflect a diverse range of experiences and perspectives. We could also avoid assumptions about shared knowledge or cultural norms. For example, when selecting texts for an English exam, we could include authors from a variety of cultural backgrounds to ensure inclusivity.

Reducing the role of high-stakes testing: We could move towards ongoing, formative assessments that track progress over time rather than relying solely on high-stakes exams. This approach reduces pressure and provides a more accurate picture of learner ability. For example, we could incorporate regular quizzes, peer reviews, and project-based assessments into the curriculum.

Offering support for EAL learners: We could use plain, accessible language in assessments and provide scaffolding, such as glossaries or translated instructions, to help EAL learners demonstrate their understanding. For example, we could allow EAL learners to use dual-language dictionaries or annotate answers in their first language.

Addressing socioeconomic barriers: We could provide equitable access to resources, such as after-school study clubs, free revision materials, or loaned technology, to ensure disadvantaged learners can prepare effectively. For example, we could run free breakfast revision sessions to give all learners a level playing field.

Challenge gender stereotypes: We could design assessment tasks that appeal to a wide range of interests and experiences, avoiding gendered framing. For example, in maths we could ensure problem-solving scenarios include examples from everyday life, rather than just sports or engineering.

Involve learners in the process: We could gather feedback from learners about their assessment experiences. This can reveal potential biases or barriers and help refine practices. For example, we could use anonymous surveys to ask learners how fair and accessible they found recent assessments.

Inclusive assessments recognise the diverse needs and abilities of all learners, ensuring that no one is unfairly disadvantaged. By diversifying formats, providing adjustments, and challenging biases, schools can create a fairer system that truly reflects learners' potential. In doing so, we foster a culture of equity, supporting every learner to succeed and thrive.

I'm now going to focus on three specific ways of making assessment more inclusive:

1. Addressing the cultural capital bias in test questions

2. Addressing differences in learners' prior knowledge

3. Addressing the anxiety of high-stakes assessments

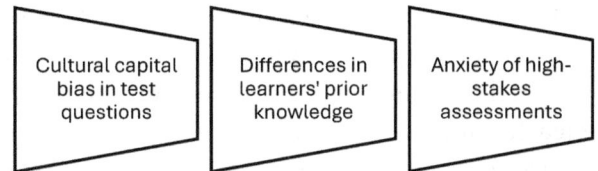

Figure 13.1 Three ways of making assessment inclusive

1. Addressing the cultural capital bias in test questions

Cultural capital bias refers to the idea that some test and exam questions favour learners from certain cultural backgrounds over others, which can disadvantage learners who do not share that background. This bias can perpetuate inequalities and contribute to achievement gaps. Addressing this issue is crucial to ensuring that assessments fairly reflect *all* learners' abilities and knowledge, not just those with social privilege.

Cultural capital refers to the values, knowledge, attitudes, and skills that learners inherit or acquire from their families and communities. This can influence their familiarity with specific contexts, references, or experiences that are often embedded in test questions. Learners from different cultural backgrounds may have varying levels of exposure to certain cultural knowledge or contexts which are implicitly assumed or expected in the wording of questions. This can disadvantage learners who are not as familiar with these references.

When questions rely heavily on specific cultural capital, learners who do not share this knowledge may struggle to understand or engage with the content, affecting their performance. This can lead to misinterpretations, disengagement, or lower self-confidence in their abilities. For example, a test question about a British historical event or a literary classic may disadvantage learners who have not had the opportunity to study these topics in detail.

In order to tackle this issue, we can:

Review test and exam content – when it's in our control to do so – to include a range of cultural perspectives and experiences. This might involve integrating global, local, and multicultural references into assessments. For instance, rather than focusing solely on British history, we might include questions that highlight contributions from a variety of cultures or global events. We might also consult with diverse members of our school community to review and revise test questions to ensure they are culturally inclusive of our cohort. We might also pilot questions with different learner groups to gauge their understanding and adjust accordingly.

Explicitly teach cultural capital to ensure learners have access to a broad and inclusive curriculum that covers a variety of cultural references, historical events, and literature. This can be achieved through literature, history, geography, and social studies lessons that incorporate diverse perspectives. This strategy might require some professional development for teachers on recognising cultural capital bias and how to teach it inclusively. Such training should cover how to diversify content, challenge stereotypes, and engage all learners in learning.

Use formative assessment to gauge understanding. This might involve implementing formative assessments throughout the year to gauge learners' understanding of different cultural contexts. This can be done through discussion-based assessments, open-ended questions, and project-based tasks that encourage learners to explore and share their cultural experiences. It might also involve using feedback from these assessments to help teachers identify areas where cultural capital bias might be present and adapt their teaching strategies accordingly.

Encourage a broad range of experiences. This might involve organising trips, guest speakers, and extracurricular activities that expose learners to diverse cultural experiences. This helps all learners build a wider range of cultural capital, which they can then draw upon in assessments. It might also involve promoting reading that represents diverse voices, authors, and perspectives to help learners gain a more well-rounded view of the world and increase their cultural capital.

Challenge stereotypes and assumptions. To do this, we might teach learners to critically engage with test content. We might encourage them to question assumptions and consider multiple perspectives when interpreting questions. This can empower learners to recognise and challenge cultural biases they may encounter in assessments. And we might incorporate discussions about cultural bias into lessons, creating a safe space where learners can discuss their experiences and explore how different cultural backgrounds can shape understanding and interpretation of test content.

Addressing cultural capital bias in test and exam questions is essential to fostering fairness and equity in the education system. By diversifying content, teaching cultural capital explicitly, and challenging biases, we can ensure that assessments provide an accurate reflection of all learners' abilities. This approach not only supports fairer outcomes but also helps to create a more inclusive educational environment where all learners feel valued and represented.

Another way to help disadvantaged learners compete more equitably in exams and other high stakes assessments is to fill gaps in their prior knowledge and skills . . .

2. Addressing differences in learners' prior knowledge

Disadvantaged learners often face significant challenges in school assessments due to limited exposure to cultural and world knowledge outside of school. These learners may lack access to experiences, resources, and opportunities that enrich their understanding of the world, which can put them at a disadvantage when it comes to school assessments that assume a certain level of prior knowledge.

Disadvantaged learners may not have been afforded the same opportunities to develop world knowledge, engage in extracurricular activities, or participate in enriching cultural experiences outside of school as their peers. This gap in cultural capital can affect their ability to access, interpret, and excel in school assessments that require a broad understanding of subjects like history, literature, science, and the arts.

Here are some practical strategies for addressing this issue:

Enrichment programmes

We can create or expand enrichment programmes that expose disadvantaged learners to a wider range of cultural, historical, and global experiences. This could include field trips to museums, art galleries, historical sites, and cultural events, as well as guest speakers from diverse backgrounds. By bringing the world into the classroom, learners can gain valuable knowledge and experiences that they might not otherwise have access to. For example, inviting local artists, authors, or scientists to speak can provide learners with direct exposure to areas of study that they may not have encountered otherwise.

Integrated curriculum

We can integrate cultural capital into the curriculum itself. This can involve using diverse texts, case studies, and historical events that reflect a range of cultural perspectives. For instance, studying literature from different cultures or discussing scientific contributions from around the world can help broaden learners' horizons. By making the curriculum more inclusive, we can provide disadvantaged learners with the same breadth of knowledge as their peers.

Extra-curricular activities

Providing access to extracurricular activities such as music, drama, sports, and clubs related to science, technology, engineering, and mathematics (STEM) can also play a critical role in building cultural capital. These activities offer learners opportunities to develop new skills, engage with peers from diverse backgrounds, and participate in projects that require teamwork and creativity. We could collaborate with community organisations to offer free or subsidised extracurricular opportunities, making these experiences more accessible to all learners.

Mentoring and support systems

Establishing mentoring programmes where disadvantaged learners are paired with peers or adults who can provide guidance and support is another effective strategy.

Mentors can offer insights into academic and non-academic pursuits, help with goal setting, and share experiences that can expand learners' horizons. Additionally, we can create study groups that encourage collaboration and peer-to-peer learning, allowing disadvantaged learners to learn from their peers who may have more cultural capital.

Professional development for teachers

Educators need to be equipped with the skills to identify and address gaps in learners' prior knowledge and skills. Professional development focused on cultural competence, differentiation, and the use of inclusive teaching strategies can help teachers better support disadvantaged learners. This might include training on how to assess and develop cultural capital within the classroom, as well as strategies for teaching in a culturally responsive manner.

Parent and community engagement

Engaging parents, families, and communities is also crucial. We can host workshops, information sessions, and community events that provide parents with resources and strategies to support their children's learning. By fostering a strong link between home and school, we can help build a supportive environment that extends beyond the classroom.

Filling gaps in disadvantaged learners' prior knowledge and cultural capital requires a multifaceted approach that involves enrichment, integration, support systems, and collaboration with the community. The goal here is not just to close achievement gaps but to empower learners with the knowledge and skills they need to thrive in an increasingly complex and interconnected world.

As well as addressing knowledge gaps, we can help prepare disadvantaged learners for high stakes assessments by teaching the study skills and coping strategies needed to prepare well and perform under pressure . . .

3. Addressing the anxiety of high-stakes assessments

Love them or hate them, exams are a fundamental part of the education system and look set to be so for the foreseeable future. And yet exams can be a source of anxiety and struggle for many learners, particularly those from disadvantaged backgrounds.

As we've seen, high-stakes assessments often assume a certain level of prior knowledge and test-taking skills that some learners may lack due to limited exposure to academic resources and experiences outside of school.

Disadvantaged learners may face other, unique barriers to exam success. These can include limited access to study resources, lack of a supportive home environment, and lower levels of cultural capital that affect their understanding of exam content and expectations. Furthermore, the pressure of high-stakes assessments can exacerbate these challenges, leading to heightened stress and anxiety. It is crucial to address these issues proactively by implementing targeted support strategies that cater to the specific needs of disadvantaged learners.

To help, we should **start preparing learners well in advance of exams**. Early identification of learners who may struggle with exams is key. We can use formative assessments, in-class quizzes, and observations to identify gaps in knowledge and skills. Once identified, these learners can be provided with tailored support, such as additional study sessions, access to targeted resources, and one-to-one tutoring if necessary. This early intervention can help mitigate the pressure of last-minute exam cramming and provide a more sustained approach to learning.

We should also **explicitly teach organisational skills**. Disadvantaged learners may not always have the same access to effective study techniques or time management strategies. We can offer lessons – perhaps in PSHE – that teach learners how to organise their study time, take effective notes, use revision aids, and approach exams methodically. These sessions can be delivered through workshops, online resources, or even peer-led initiatives. The goal is to equip learners with the tools they need to independently prepare for exams and manage their workload effectively.

We should **promote a supportive and positive exam culture** that includes mental well-being strategies. This could involve sessions on stress management, mindfulness techniques, and physical activities that help alleviate anxiety. Additionally, providing a calm and supportive exam environment can improve focus and performance.

Engaging parents and families is vital in preparing learners for exams. We should **maintain open lines of communication with parents**, providing them with resources and strategies they can use to support their child's exam preparation at home. This might include setting realistic expectations, creating a study-friendly environment, and monitoring progress. Regular parent-teacher meetings can also keep parents informed about their child's progress and any additional support they may need.

High-stakes assessments can be daunting for any learner, but they present additional challenges for learners who may already struggle with language barriers, unfamiliar content, and the pressure to perform. When faced with exams that include complex language or content that is outside their usual experience, these learners are at risk of experiencing panic, anxiety, and underperformance.

As we've already seen, disadvantaged learners may also lack the cultural capital and linguistic resources that other learners take for granted, which can make understanding exam questions and content more challenging. This can lead to panic, confusion, and disengagement during assessments. Without appropriate coping strategies, these learners might struggle to demonstrate their true ability, which can impact their overall academic performance. To support these learners, schools need to equip them with effective strategies that build resilience and confidence in handling high-pressure exam situations.

Here are some practical coping strategies we could teach . . .

To help prepare for exams

- **Break down exam content**: Before the exam, we could break down the exam content into manageable parts, identifying key topics and areas where learners might need extra support. This can help learners feel more prepared and less overwhelmed. For example, if an exam includes a complex text, teachers can pre-teach vocabulary or essential background knowledge to ensure that learners can understand and engage with the material.

- **Teach study skills**: We could teach learners specific study skills such as note-taking, summarisation, and keyword identification. These strategies can help learners prioritise important information and focus their revision effectively. For instance, using mind maps or flashcards can aid in organising and retaining information.

- **Walk through exam hall routines**: We could ensure learners have practised the logistical aspects of sitting high stakes assessments so there is no uncertainty or apprehension about where to go, how to enter the exam hall, where to sit, where to find key information, and so on.

To help cope during the exam

- **Practice relaxation techniques**: We could incorporate relaxation techniques such as deep breathing exercises, visualisation, and progressive muscle relaxation into exam preparation. These techniques can help learners manage anxiety and stay focused during the exam. For example, encouraging learners to take a few deep breaths before starting an exam can help calm their nerves and improve concentration.

- **Teach exam-specific strategies**: We could provide learners with strategies specific to handling exam questions. For instance, when faced with an unfamiliar question, we could encourage learners to read it multiple times, underline key words, and break down complex instructions into simpler parts. This approach can prevent panic and promote a more thoughtful and methodical response.

- **Practice under exam conditions**: We could use mock exams and practice questions to simulate exam conditions. This can help learners become accustomed to the time pressure and the format of high-stakes assessments. Feedback from these practice sessions can also help learners understand their weaknesses and areas for improvement.

To help reflect and learn after the exam

- **Reflect on and analyse exam performance**: After exams, we could ask learners to reflect on their performance and identify areas where they felt particularly stressed or uncertain. This reflection can be facilitated through group discussions, individual conversations with teachers, or written reflections. Understanding their own stress triggers can help learners develop personalised strategies for coping in future assessments.

- **Provide constructive feedback**: We could give learners specific, constructive feedback on their performance. This helps them understand what they did well and where they can improve. Positive reinforcement and encouragement can boost confidence and motivate learners to persevere through future challenges.

At all times

- **Create a supportive classroom culture**: We should foster a classroom environment where learners feel comfortable sharing their concerns and seeking support. Encourage peer collaboration and study groups where learners can discuss their concerns and strategies with each other. This peer support can provide reassurance and help learners develop a sense of belonging and shared purpose.

Teaching coping strategies for disadvantaged learners in high-stakes assessments requires a proactive and multi-faceted approach. By preparing learners in advance, teaching specific exam-related skills, and fostering a supportive classroom environment, we can help reduce anxiety and improve performance. Equipping learners with these strategies not only helps them to succeed academically, but it also builds essential life skills that can contribute to their overall well-being and resilience in the face of future challenges.

Self-evaluation

Having read about inclusive assessment, put the theory into practice by answering the following self-evaluative questions:

1. How well do you understand the concept of cultural capital bias in assessments, and how might it impact learners from different cultural backgrounds?
2. What strategies can be implemented to support learners with language barriers in assessments, and how effective do you think these strategies could be?
3. What role do socio-economic disparities play in academic assessments, and how can schools address these challenges to ensure fairer outcomes?
4. How can we ensure that learners with special educational needs and disabilities (SEND) have equal opportunities to demonstrate their abilities in assessments?
5. What are some practical ways that assessments can be designed to minimise gender bias and promote fairness for all students?

6. In what ways do traditional assessments prioritise certain types of intelligence, and how can a more inclusive approach better cater to diverse learning strengths?

7. Reflecting on the examples of inclusive assessment practices, which methods do you think could be most effective in your own educational context?

8. How can diversifying the assessment formats (e.g., oral presentations, group projects) help to reduce bias and offer a more accurate reflection of learners' potential?

9. What can schools do to address the anxiety surrounding high-stakes assessments, particularly for disadvantaged or marginalised learners?

10. How can teachers and schools ensure that assessments are designed to address differences in learners' prior knowledge and cultural capital, and why is this important?

14 The SEND system

SEND runs through this book – and indeed the whole series – like the letters in a stick of rock. But in this chapter, I'd like to conduct a deeper dive into the SEND system . . .

Under the Equality Act 2010, schools have a legal duty to make reasonable adjustments to ensure disabled learners can access education on an equal footing with their peers. This anticipatory duty means schools must proactively consider and address potential barriers before they arise. But what exactly is 'reasonable'? Well, the factors to consider include:

- The specific needs of the learner
- The resources and size of the school
- Health and safety implications
- The practicality and effectiveness of the adjustment
- The impact on maintaining academic and extracurricular standards

Reasonable adjustments can involve changes to policies, the physical environment, or the provision of additional aids. For example:

- A timetable adjustment that allows learners with learning difficulties to receive extra support without missing core lessons
- A seating plan adjustment to ensure a learner with a hearing impairment is located near the teacher to aid lip-reading and hearing
- Flexible uniform rules to accommodate sensory needs or medical conditions
- Alternative sanctions to replace exclusions when behaviour stems from a disability

Inclusion starts with understanding the unique needs of the school community. Knowing who our learners are – and anticipating their future needs – helps create a welcoming and accessible environment for all. This extends beyond learners to families, staff, and the broader school community.

Building an inclusive environment requires flexibility and creativity. Small changes, such as alternative snack policies for learners with diabetes or providing sensory tools for regulation, can make a significant difference.

All teachers must also adapt their teaching methods to respond to the diverse needs of their learners. According to the Teachers' Standards, this includes:

- Differentiating effectively to enable all learners to learn
- Understanding how physical, social, and intellectual factors influence learning
- Using distinctive approaches to engage and support learners with special educational needs, disabilities, or English as an additional language

Inclusion isn't just about academic adjustments, though; it's about the whole school experience. For example, we should consider if:

- Extracurricular activities are accessible to learners with additional needs
- Events like school fairs or discos include provisions for all learners
- Junior leadership opportunities are open to diverse groups of learners
- Learners with additional needs are active participants in representing the school

You may also wish to consider the following practical strategies for supporting learners with specific SEND . . .

Adapting lessons for cognition and learning needs

Learners with cognition and learning needs often require differentiated instruction and additional support to thrive. Effective strategies include:

- Breaking tasks into smaller, manageable steps
- Providing scaffolds such as writing frames or worked examples
- Offering additional time for task completion and concept rehearsal
- Adjusting curriculum content to focus on key priorities

Supporting executive function – such as working memory, flexible thinking, and self-control – is also crucial. Tools like voice recorders, alternative formats for output, and technology-based solutions can help learners manage cognitive demands.

Addressing communication and interaction needs

Learners with communication needs may struggle with speech production, receptive or expressive language, or social communication. We can support these learners by:

- Pre-teaching subject-specific vocabulary with visual aids
- Sequencing instructions clearly and providing additional processing time
- Limiting background noise and incorporating visual cues
- Using paired talk and sentence starters to rehearse responses

Clear communication fosters understanding and builds confidence, enabling learners to engage fully with the curriculum and their peers.

Supporting social, emotional, and mental health (SEMH)

Schools play a vital role in promoting positive mental health. Mentally healthy classrooms provide safe spaces where learners feel valued and understood. Strategies include:

- Creating opportunities for learners to express worries and feelings
- Celebrating unique strengths and talents
- Teaching mental health awareness and coping skills
- Providing self-regulation resources like safe spaces and sensory tools

Strong relationships between learners and staff underpin effective SEMH support. We must be attuned to our learners' mental well-being and know when and how to seek additional help.

Addressing physical and sensory needs

Physical and sensory difficulties often require tailored adjustments to ensure accessibility. Examples include:

- Providing assistive technologies such as screen readers or adapted keyboards
- Enlarging text and offering alternative formats for resources
- Flexible seating arrangements and modified tools to promote independence
- Considering fatigue and pacing lessons accordingly

Embedding routines for success

Well-established rules and routines are essential in inclusive classrooms. They create consistency, reduce anxiety, and support smooth transitions. Clear expectations and structured plans help all learners, particularly those with additional needs, to navigate the school day successfully.

Effective lesson planning starts with knowing your learners' starting points. Adaptive plans should:

- Honour prior learning and experiences
- Include high expectations for all learners
- Identify appropriate scaffolds and resources
- Integrate opportunities for teacher modelling, guided practice, and independent work

Lessons should be flexible and responsive, adapting to emerging needs as they arise. This dynamic approach ensures all learners can engage meaningfully and achieve their potential.

Inclusive education is about removing barriers and creating opportunities for every learner. By fostering collaboration, celebrating diversity, and employing adaptive strategies, schools can build environments where every learner can thrive. Inclusion is not just a legal obligation but a moral imperative to ensure equity and excellence for all.

The elephant in the room: Is the SEND system broken?

The special educational needs and disabilities (SEND) system in England is a lifeline for learners requiring additional support. However, there is growing consensus among educators, parents, and policymakers that the system is under immense strain, leaving many learners and their families feeling under-served. While the system is not entirely broken, it is undeniably buckling under the weight of growing demand, funding pressures, and administrative complexity.

The statistics speak for themselves: The number of children with Education, Health, and Care Plans (EHCPs) has risen by 71% in six years. By 2024, 5% of all learners in England had an EHCP, with countless others who failed to meet the EHCP threshold still requiring significant support.

Despite additional funding being funnelled into SEND provision, delays in assessment remain – at time of writing – unacceptably long, children's needs are going unmet, and parents are being left exhausted and exasperated by a system that sometimes feels designed to obstruct rather than support. Schools, families, and local councils may disagree on the specifics, but they are united in one belief: The current system is not fit for purpose.

Adding to the urgency is a looming financial deadline. Since 2020, councils in England have been able to park around £3.3 billion of SEND overspend 'off the books' thanks to an accounting loophole known as the statutory override. But this is set to end in 2026, and when it does, local authorities will face a financial reckoning unless drastic action is taken.

Here, we'll explore the challenges and some practical steps for improvement.

Key challenges facing the SEND system

1. Insufficient funding

One of the most significant barriers is the chronic underfunding of SEND provision. Schools and local authorities often lack the resources required to meet the needs of all eligible learners, leading to delays in support and, in some cases, unmet needs. For example, many schools struggle to provide one-to-one support for learners with Education, Health and Care Plans (EHCPs), let alone those who require help but don't qualify for formal plans.

2. Lengthy and bureaucratic processes

Securing an EHCP is often a slow and cumbersome process, leaving families frustrated and children unsupported for extended periods. The process can involve extensive paperwork, repeated assessments, and a lack of transparency about decisions. For example, parents frequently report waiting over a year for an EHCP, only to face additional battles if the plan is deemed inadequate.

3. Inconsistent provision across regions

SEND provision is often described as a postcode lottery, with significant disparities in the quality and availability of support depending on where a family lives. This inconsistency undermines the principle of equitable access to education. For example, some local authorities have more robust specialist support teams, while others struggle to meet even basic needs due to staffing shortages.

4. Pressure on mainstream schools

With specialist provision oversubscribed, more children with SEND are being placed in mainstream schools. While inclusion is a laudable goal, many mainstream settings lack the training, staffing, and resources to provide adequate support, creating challenges for learners, teachers, and classmates alike. For example, teachers in mainstream classrooms often report feeling ill-equipped to manage the complex needs of SEND learners without additional training or support staff.

5. Impact on families

Families often bear the brunt of systemic failings, facing emotional and financial pressures as they navigate a system that can feel adversarial and exhausting. Many parents resort to costly legal action to secure the support their child needs. For example, the rise in SEND tribunals highlights the extent to which families feel compelled to fight for basic entitlements.

So, what can we do to fix the SEND system?

1. Increase funding for SEND provision

It's perhaps the most obvious answer but the least likely to happen – and it's certainly a solution out of our direct control. But adequate funding is essential to ensure schools and local authorities can meet the growing demand for SEND services. This includes investing in specialist staff, resources, and training for mainstream schools. The government should therefore allocate ring-fenced budgets for SEND provision and regularly review funding levels to match demand.

2. Streamline the EHCP process

The EHCP system should be simplified and made more efficient. Clearer guidelines, faster assessment timelines, and reduced bureaucracy would alleviate pressure on families and local authorities alike. One suggestion would be for the government to introduce digital platforms to streamline applications and improve communication between stakeholders, ensuring greater transparency and accountability.

3. Address regional inequalities

To eliminate the postcode lottery, national standards for SEND provision could be established and monitored. This would ensure consistent quality and access across all local authorities. One tangible strategy: Create a national framework for SEND services, while allowing flexibility for local needs and innovation.

4. Invest in specialist provision

Expanding specialist schools and support units would reduce pressure on mainstream schools and ensure learners with complex needs receive tailored support. A suggested solution: Increase funding for new specialist schools and ensure existing settings are adequately staffed and resourced.

5. Enhance training for teachers

All teachers, whether in mainstream or specialist settings, should receive comprehensive training on SEND. This would build confidence and competence, ensuring all learners receive high-quality support. To help, we could incorporate mandatory SEND modules into initial teacher training and provide ongoing professional development.

6. Strengthen collaboration with families

Parents and carers are key partners in their children's education, yet they often feel sidelined. Greater collaboration would lead to better outcomes and reduce the adversarial nature of the current system. A solution? To introduce regular consultation with families and establish parent forums to co-design local SEND strategies.

Another route towards meaningful improvement is curriculum reform. Across the developed world, there has been a marked rise in autism, ADHD, and mental health challenges among young people. While this trend can't be pinned solely on domestic education policy, it's clear that some decisions – such as the shift to exam-heavy GCSEs and cuts to school budgets – have made classrooms less flexible and less welcoming for learners with additional needs. A more inclusive curriculum, combined with further research into the root causes of these trends, could therefore be a solution worth considering.

In sum, the SEND system is not beyond repair, but it does require urgent reform. By addressing funding shortfalls, reducing bureaucracy, and investing in training and resources, we can create a system that works for all learners. Crucially, these changes must be informed by the voices of families and educators, ensuring that support is not only adequate but also equitable and effective.

Every child deserves the chance to thrive, and fixing the SEND system is a moral and practical imperative that cannot wait.

Self-evaluation

Having read about SEND, put the theory into practice by answering the following self-evaluative questions:

1. What are the key principles of reasonable adjustments as outlined under the Equality Act 2010, and how can these principles be applied in a school setting?
2. Reflect on the factors schools need to consider when determining what constitutes a 'reasonable adjustment'. Which of these do you think is most challenging to implement and why?
3. How does understanding the unique needs of learners contribute to building a more inclusive school environment?
4. In what ways can you effectively differentiate your teaching to meet the needs of students with special educational needs and disabilities (SEND)?
5. What are some practical adjustments that can be made to support learners with cognitive and learning needs, and how would these adjustments benefit their learning experience?

6. How can schools foster a school culture that supports the mental health and well-being of learners with SEND? What specific strategies can be implemented?

7. How can you make extracurricular activities more accessible to students with additional needs?

8. What are the key challenges facing the SEND system, and what changes do you think are necessary to address these challenges effectively?

9. Reflecting on the suggested improvements for the SEND system, which of them do you think would have the most immediate impact on students' experiences and why?

10. How can teachers and school leaders improve their collaboration with families to support SEND learners, and what benefits might this have for the students?

PART FOUR
Oracy and reading for pleasure

15 Oracy and inclusion

As we discovered in the examples of Thomas and Tommy, success at school is not all about exams. Thomas told us that some people are more confident and able to explain themselves than others. Thomas said he got his confidence from his dad. He said he feels like he belongs everywhere and never feels excluded or isolated. He is proud of who he is and can speak his mind. He knows how to talk to teachers and people at his dad's work. But some young people, like Tommy, talk the same way to teachers as they do their friends, and it holds them back because many people conflate articulacy and confidence with ability or intellect.

Another dimension to inclusion, therefore, underpinning lesson planning, teaching, and assessment, is oracy – the power of spoken language and communication. After all, if belonging is about all learners feeling valued and respected and included, how can we achieve this if learners are unable to express themselves and have their voices heard?

Oracy refers to the ability to express oneself effectively and to understand spoken language in various contexts. It encompasses the skills required to communicate clearly, listen actively, and engage thoughtfully in dialogue. Oracy is as vital to education as literacy and numeracy, yet it is sometimes neglected in favour of these more traditional pillars. If we are to equip young people with the tools they need to succeed in life, we must place oracy at the heart of our classrooms.

It might be helpful to deconstruct oracy into four component parts:

1. *Physical skills*

    This includes voice projection, clarity of speech, and the use of non-verbal communication such as gestures, posture, and eye contact. These are the tools that make a speaker's message accessible and engaging.

2. *Linguistic skills*

    These involve the vocabulary and grammar necessary to construct coherent sentences, as well as rhetorical techniques like repetition, metaphor, and analogy, which enhance persuasiveness and impact.

3. *Cognitive skills*

   Effective communication requires the ability to organise one's thoughts, plan a logical structure, and adapt to different audiences and purposes. This includes critical thinking and the capacity to evaluate and respond to others' contributions.

4. *Social and emotional skills*

   Communication is fundamentally about connection. Oracy involves listening attentively, showing empathy, managing turn-taking, and responding to others in a way that builds rapport and respect. These skills foster collaboration and mutual understanding.

Why does oracy matter?

In today's world, the ability to speak well is an essential life skill. Whether presenting in a formal setting, contributing to a group discussion, or navigating everyday social interactions, oracy empowers individuals to express themselves confidently and persuasively. Giving learners frequent opportunities to express themselves and take part in discussions helps to develop their cognitive processes and gives them a chance to have their views heard. Being heard, in turn, helps build self-awareness and self-confidence.

Educational outcomes

Research shows that strong oracy skills correlate with improved academic outcomes across all subjects. Discussing ideas aloud helps learners to process and retain information, while debate and dialogue sharpen their reasoning and deepen understanding.

Social mobility

Oracy levels the playing field. Learners from disadvantaged backgrounds often enter school with less developed verbal skills, yet these are crucial for success in interviews, higher education, and the workplace. Explicitly teaching oracy can help bridge this gap.

Preparation for the future

Employers consistently rank communication skills as among the most desirable attributes in prospective employees. In an economy increasingly driven by collaboration and innovation, the ability to articulate ideas clearly and work effectively with others is crucial to future success.

Civic participation

Oracy underpins democracy. This is a grand statement, I know, but in order to participate in public life, individuals must be able to articulate their views, engage in debate, and listen to differing perspectives. Teaching oracy equips young people with the tools needed to become active, informed citizens and therefore to play a full part in democracy.

Why do some disadvantaged learners lack oracy skills?

Society does not operate on a level playing field. From their earliest days, children's experiences diverge sharply based on their family's socio-economic status, shaping their confidence, articulacy, and ability to navigate the world. These disparities are not rooted in innate ability but in the vastly different environments and opportunities that rich and poor children encounter.

So, what is it that makes affluent children more confident and articulate, while their disadvantaged peers often struggle to assert themselves?

1. A wealth of early experiences

Affluent children are often immersed in a wide range of enriching experiences from a young age. Visits to museums, theatres, libraries, and cultural events expose them to new ideas, foster curiosity, and help them feel at ease in unfamiliar environments. They become comfortable navigating different social and intellectual spaces, building a reservoir of knowledge and experiences to draw upon in conversation.

In contrast, disadvantaged children may have fewer opportunities for such exposure. Economic constraints and limited access to transport or childcare mean these experiences are often out of reach. As a result, poorer children may lack the social and cultural capital that their wealthier peers take for granted.

2. Language-rich environments

Language is a key determinant of confidence and articulacy. Research shows that by the age of 3, children from wealthier households have heard significantly more words than those from disadvantaged backgrounds. This disparity, known as the "word gap", has profound implications.

In affluent homes, children are often engaged in rich, reciprocal conversations. Parents may use sophisticated vocabulary, ask open-ended questions, and encourage their children to articulate their thoughts and feelings. These interactions help children develop a robust vocabulary and the ability to express complex ideas.

Disadvantaged children, by contrast, may grow up in environments where talk is more functional and less frequent. This is not a reflection of parental care or love but often a consequence of economic pressures. Parents working multiple jobs or coping with stress may have less time or energy for extended dialogue. As a result, these children may start school with a smaller vocabulary and less practice in using language to reason or explain.

3. Social confidence and self-belief

Affluent children are often raised with a sense of entitlement – not arrogance, but an underlying belief that they have a right to be heard and a place in the world. This confidence is cultivated through opportunities to participate in structured activities such as drama clubs, sports teams, and leadership roles, as well as through positive reinforcement at home and in school.

Disadvantaged children, on the other hand, may experience a world that feels hostile or dismissive. They may internalise low expectations, shaped by societal biases or their own encounters with inequality. Fear of failure or ridicule can make them hesitant to put themselves forward, reinforcing a cycle of under-confidence.

4. Familiarity with formal contexts

Rich children are often introduced early to the unwritten rules of formal situations. They learn how to make eye contact, shake hands confidently, and engage in polite conversation with adults. They practise adapting their speech to suit different audiences, whether speaking to a teacher, a peer, or a professional.

Disadvantaged children may have fewer opportunities to practise these skills. They might find formal settings intimidating because they are unfamiliar, leading to a sense of alienation and a reluctance to participate.

5. Networks and role models

Affluent children are often surrounded by role models who demonstrate confidence and articulacy in action. Parents and their social networks may include professionals who model effective communication and problem-solving. These children grow up seeing their future selves reflected in successful, articulate adults.

Disadvantaged children, by contrast, may lack access to such networks. They might not see people like them in positions of influence or hear their own dialects and accents valued in formal or professional contexts. This absence of relatable role models can make it harder for them to imagine themselves as confident, articulate individuals.

6. The hidden curriculum of social class

Affluent children often benefit from what sociologists call the "hidden curriculum" – the unspoken lessons about how to succeed in society. They learn to speak with authority, ask for help without fear, and navigate systems with ease. These skills, while not explicitly taught, are passed down through everyday interactions and experiences.

For disadvantaged children, the hidden curriculum is often inaccessible. They may not know how to advocate for themselves or feel entitled to challenge authority. This lack of cultural capital can leave them at a disadvantage in competitive environments such as schools, workplaces, and interviews.

A call to action . . .

The confidence and articulacy of affluent children are not innate gifts but the product of environments rich in opportunity, language, and positive reinforcement. Conversely, the struggles of disadvantaged children to assert themselves stem not from a lack of potential but from a lack of access to these same advantages.

Schools, therefore, have a vital role to play in levelling the playing field. By prioritising oracy, broadening learners' horizons, and teaching the unwritten rules of success, we can ensure that all children – regardless of background – are equipped to thrive. The goal is not to mimic privilege but to unlock potential, creating a society where every child's voice is heard and valued.

What can we do to help disadvantaged learners develop oracy skills?

It is a troubling reality that society often equates confidence and articulacy with ability and aptitude. Affluent children, with their greater exposure to diverse experiences and enriched language environments, are often more comfortable navigating new situations and expressing their ideas. Disadvantaged children, by contrast, may lack these advantages, not because they lack ability, but because they have had fewer opportunities to develop the skills and self-assurance that affluent children take for granted.

Schools can play a vital role in addressing this imbalance. By intentionally building the confidence, articulacy, and social capital of disadvantaged children, we can ensure that talent, not background, determines success.

Here's how we might do it . . .

Step 1: Prioritise oracy across the curriculum

Disadvantaged children often enter school with a limited vocabulary and less experience of using language to articulate their ideas. By prioritising oracy – the ability to speak well and listen actively – we can help these learners find their voice. To do this, we can:

- Create opportunities for structured talk: We can use activities like debates, presentations, and collaborative problem-solving to give all learners the chance to practise speaking in a range of contexts.

- Teach the language of success: We can explicitly teach academic and professional vocabulary and show learners how to adapt their speech for different audiences and purposes.

- Model and scaffold: We can use sentence stems and discussion frameworks to help learners structure their responses and build confidence over time.

Step 2: Build social confidence through exposure

As I've already explained, affluent children often benefit from exposure to a wide variety of environments, from museums and theatres to professional workplaces. Schools can replicate this exposure to build the social confidence of disadvantaged children. In practice, this might mean that we:

- Broaden cultural experiences: We can provide access to trips, performances, and workshops that enrich learners' horizons and spark curiosity.
- Create authentic experiences: We can use role-play and simulations, such as mock interviews or workplace scenarios, to help learners practise navigating formal settings.
- Invite guest speakers: We can bring in professionals from a range of industries to inspire learners and model effective communication.

Step 3: Develop self-belief and growth mindsets

Disadvantaged children often face barriers of low self-esteem, exacerbated by societal biases that equate quietness with inability. Schools must actively counter these messages. To help, we can:

- Celebrate effort, not just achievement: We can recognise and reward learners for their progress and perseverance, emphasising that ability grows with effort.
- Challenge stereotypes: We can use examples and role models to show learners that success is not limited by background.
- Explicitly teach self-belief: We can use positive affirmations, reflection, and coaching to help learners recognise their own potential.

Step 4: Teach code-switching skills

Many disadvantaged children speak in non-standard dialects at home and may struggle to adapt to the formal language required in academic or professional settings. Teaching code-switching empowers them to navigate these contexts without devaluing their cultural identity. To help, we can:

- Respect home languages: We can validate and celebrate the linguistic diversity learners bring with them.

- Explicitly teach formal registers: We can show learners how and when to use Standard English, providing plenty of opportunities to practise.

- Encourage pride in adaptability: We can frame code-switching as a skill that broadens their horizons and increases their agency.

Step 5: Provide opportunities for leadership

Leadership roles encourage learners to take responsibility, develop confidence, and practise articulating their ideas. Affluent children often gain these experiences outside school, but schools can provide them for all. To help, we can:

- Create classroom roles: We can assign responsibilities such as leading group discussions or presenting findings to the class.

- Encourage participation in clubs and councils: We can ensure disadvantaged learners are supported to take part in extracurricular activities that build leadership and teamwork skills.

- Offer mentoring programmes: We can pair learners with older peers or professionals who can guide them and boost their confidence.

Step 6: Ensure fair access to opportunities

Affluent children often benefit from networks of support and guidance that help them seize opportunities. Schools must act as a bridge for disadvantaged learners. We should therefore:

- Provide career education: We can offer workshops, mentoring, and exposure to careers that disadvantaged learners may not have considered.

- Support applications and interviews: We can teach learners how to write CVs, complete application forms, and present themselves confidently in interviews.

- Offer financial support: We can ensure no learner is excluded from opportunities due to cost, providing bursaries or covering expenses where necessary.

Step 7: Foster critical thinking and independence

Affluent children are often encouraged to question, challenge, and explore ideas from an early age. Schools can help disadvantaged learners develop these same habits of mind. To help, we can:

- Use open-ended tasks: We can design activities that encourage learners to think deeply, evaluate evidence, and justify their reasoning.

- Encourage questioning: We can create a classroom culture where curiosity is celebrated and learners feel safe asking questions.

- Teach problem-solving skills: We can provide frameworks and strategies for tackling complex problems independently.

A caveat . . .

While schools can do much to level the playing field, societal inequalities must also be addressed. We might not be able to change the world, but we can act as advocates for change by:

- *Engaging families*: We can work with parents and carers to support learners' confidence and articulacy at home. We can provide workshops, resources, and guidance to help families navigate the education system.

- **Challenging biases**: We can train staff to recognise and counteract unconscious biases that might disadvantage quieter or less articulate learners.

- *Collaborating with communities*: We can partner with local organisations and employers to create opportunities for all learners.

Self-evaluation

Having read about oracy, put the theory into practice by answering the following self-evaluative questions:

1. How would you explain the concept of oracy to someone unfamiliar with it? What are its key components?

2. Why do you think oracy is considered as essential to education as literacy and numeracy?

3. What are some of the primary reasons disadvantaged learners may lack oracy skills compared to their more affluent peers?

4. How do the differences in early language exposure and cultural experiences between affluent and disadvantaged children affect their oracy development?

5. Reflecting on the suggested steps to support disadvantaged learners, which strategies do you think would be most effective in improving oracy skills in your context?

6. How can you foster social confidence in your disadvantaged learners, and why is this important for their oracy development?

7. What role does teaching code-switching play in supporting disadvantaged learners, and how can this skill be effectively taught in a classroom?

8. How can schools promote a growth mindset to help disadvantaged learners overcome barriers to effective communication?

9. In what ways can providing student leadership opportunities contribute to the development of oracy skills in all learners, especially those from disadvantaged backgrounds?

10. Based on this chapter, what are some specific actions you can take to level the playing field for disadvantaged learners in terms of oracy skills? How might these actions influence their future success?

16 Oracy – the road to equity

As we've seen, teaching oracy is vital for all young people, but it holds particular significance for disadvantaged learners. For these learners, oracy is more than a skill – it is a lifeline, a tool to unlock opportunities and bridge the gap between potential and attainment. If we are serious about addressing educational inequality, we must make oracy a central pillar of our teaching. Oracy is the road to equity.

Why? Because disadvantaged learners often enter school with less developed verbal skills compared to their more affluent peers. Children from less advantaged backgrounds are exposed to fewer words and a narrower range of vocabulary in their early years. This 'language gap' impacts their ability to articulate thoughts, engage with academic content, and build social connections.

But, by explicitly teaching oracy, we can begin to close this gap. Through structured opportunities to speak, listen, and engage in dialogue, we can provide disadvantaged learners with the linguistic tools they need to access the curriculum and thrive in education.

And it's not just about language capability; it's about confidence, too . . .

Disadvantaged learners often lack the confidence to express themselves in formal or unfamiliar settings. This lack of self-assurance can reinforce a sense of exclusion and limit their aspirations. But oracy teaching can build confidence by equipping learners with the skills to communicate effectively, whether presenting to an audience, answering questions in class, or navigating a job interview.

By developing their oracy skills, we can empower disadvantaged learners to find their voice, articulate their ambitions, and believe in their ability to succeed . . . and we can begin to break the cycle of disadvantage . . .

Education is often described as the great leveller, yet for too many disadvantaged learners, the odds remain stacked against them. Oracy teaching can help break this cycle. Effective communication is a cornerstone of social mobility, opening doors to higher education, meaningful employment, and active participation in society.

Without strong oracy skills, many disadvantaged learners are unable to compete on an equal footing with their peers. By prioritising oracy, we ensure that every learner, regardless of background, has the chance to succeed.

As such, oracy is not an optional extra; rather, it is fundamental to learning. Speaking and listening provide the foundation for reading and writing. Classroom talk helps learners to clarify their thinking, explore ideas, and deepen their understanding of complex concepts. And, for disadvantaged learners, oracy is particularly important because it provides a gateway to the curriculum. Many disadvantaged learners struggle to access academic language and grapple with unfamiliar vocabulary. By teaching them how to use and understand sophisticated language, we can give them the tools needed to engage fully with their education.

Disadvantaged learners often face barriers when transitioning to the world of work or further education. As I've already said, many employers regard communication skills as essential, yet many young people enter the workforce unprepared. Explicit oracy teaching can help ensure disadvantaged learners leave school with the ability to speak clearly, listen actively, and engage professionally. These are the skills they will need to succeed in interviews, collaborate with colleagues, and advocate for themselves in all areas of life.

What does this look like in practice?

Here are my top 5 tips for using oracy as a road to equity:

1. Teach code-switching to enable learners to speak appropriately and with confidence in a range of situations

2. Teach debating skills to enable learners to engage in discussions and articulate their views with diplomacy

3. Teach rhetoric and prosody to enable learners to speak convincingly and powerfully to argue their views

4. Teach storytelling techniques to enable learners to narrate their own lives and the lives of others

5. Deploy dialogic teaching and modelling in the classroom to make oracy an integral part of the curriculum

Let's look at each in turn . . .

1. Teach code-switching to enable learners to speak appropriately and with confidence in a range of situations

Code-switching is the ability to shift between different styles of language depending on the context, audience, or purpose. It allows individuals to adapt their speech to suit formal and informal settings, demonstrating an understanding of social norms and expectations. For disadvantaged learners, teaching code-switching is particularly important because it equips them with the tools to navigate a range of environments, from the classroom to the workplace, and to participate confidently in society.

At its heart, code-switching involves choosing the right register, tone, and vocabulary for a specific context. It might mean using Standard English in a formal setting such as an interview and then shifting to a more colloquial style when chatting with friends.

This linguistic flexibility is not about erasing or undermining a learner's own language or dialect; rather, it is about empowering them to add another 'code' to their repertoire. Code-switching is a skill that allows learners to preserve their cultural identity while accessing opportunities in settings where Standard English is expected.

For disadvantaged learners, the ability to code-switch can be transformative. Here's why:

BRIDGING THE GAP BETWEEN HOME AND SCHOOL

Many disadvantaged learners use non-standard dialects or regional accents at home, which can differ significantly from the language of education. Without explicit guidance, they may struggle to adapt to the formal register required in academic writing or classroom discussions. Teaching code-switching helps learners understand when and how to use Standard English without invalidating their own language. It bridges the gap between their lived experiences and the expectations of the school environment, fostering a sense of belonging and reducing the risk of alienation.

ACCESSING THE CURRICULUM

Academic success often depends on mastering the formal language of instruction. From exam questions to essay writing, learners are expected to use Standard English fluently and accurately. For disadvantaged learners, this can present a barrier. By teaching code-switching, we demystify academic language and give learners the tools they need to access the curriculum fully, ensuring that their ideas and insights are not lost due to linguistic obstacles.

PREPARING FOR PROFESSIONAL ENVIRONMENTS

In the workplace, the ability to adapt one's communication style is a critical skill. Employers often expect a level of formality and professionalism that may be unfamiliar to learners from disadvantaged backgrounds. By teaching code-switching, we prepare learners to succeed in interviews, collaborate effectively with colleagues, and present themselves with confidence in professional settings. This is particularly crucial for disadvantaged learners, who may not have access to the informal mentoring that teaches these skills in other contexts.

EMPOWERING LEARNERS WITH CHOICE

Code-switching is ultimately about empowerment. It gives learners the agency to decide how they wish to present themselves in different settings. Rather than feeling 'trapped' by the norms of one linguistic style, they can move fluidly between different codes, preserving their identity while meeting the expectations of various audiences.

That's the why, now the how . . .

Teaching code-switching involves more than just correcting grammar or pronunciation – it requires a sensitive and inclusive approach.

This begins by valuing and respecting the language and dialects learners bring with them. In practice, we need to show learners that their home language is an important part of their identity and a strength to be celebrated.

Next, we need to help learners to recognise the different demands of formal and informal settings. In practice, we can use examples to illustrate how language shifts depending on the audience and purpose. We also need to create scenarios where learners can practise using formal and informal registers. Role-playing activities such as job interviews or debates are particularly effective.

As teachers, we also need to model code-switching in our own speech, making it clear when we are using a formal register and why.

We also need to provide gentle guidance rather than criticism whenever learners make a mistake. We should emphasise the value of learning an additional 'code' rather than rejecting their existing way of speaking.

To conclude, code-switching is not about conforming to rigid linguistic norms; it is about giving disadvantaged learners the confidence and flexibility to navigate diverse contexts. By teaching this skill, we empower learners to succeed in school, the workplace, and society, while preserving the richness of their linguistic heritage. Code-switching is a powerful tool for social mobility and inclusion – a step towards ensuring that every learner, regardless of background, can find their voice and fulfil their potential.

Self-evaluation

Here are five self-evaluation questions to consider before you move on:

1. Can I clearly explain what code-switching is and how it empowers learners in both formal and informal settings?

2. Do I understand why it is essential to respect and celebrate the language and dialects learners bring with them when teaching code-switching?

3. How confident am I in identifying and addressing the linguistic gap between learners' home language and the formal language required in academic or professional settings?

4. Am I able to design activities, such as role-playing scenarios or discussions, to help learners practice using different registers and communication styles effectively?

5. How well can I provide constructive feedback on learners' language use in a way that emphasises growth and inclusion, rather than criticism or correction?

2. Teach debating skills to enable learners to engage in discussions and articulate their views with diplomacy

Speaking confidently is a vital skill that can transform a learner's life, enabling them to express themselves clearly, engage in meaningful dialogue, and seize opportunities. For many, however, public speaking or even everyday debate and discussion can be daunting.

Here are some practical strategies for teaching learners to speak confidently in various situations.

CREATE A SAFE AND SUPPORTIVE ENVIRONMENT

Confidence begins with feeling safe. Learners are unlikely to take risks or practise speaking if they fear ridicule or criticism. Therefore, we should establish ground rules for respectful listening and constructive feedback in the classroom. We should also model vulnerability by sharing our own experiences of learning to speak confidently, showing that mistakes are part of growth. And we should celebrate all attempts, no matter how small, to build learners' self-esteem.

TEACH THE FUNDAMENTALS OF EFFECTIVE SPEAKING

Before learners can speak confidently, they need to understand what makes effective communication. Therefore, we should teach voice control: Encourage learners to project their voice and speak clearly, avoiding mumbling or whispering. Breathing exercises can help them manage nerves and control their volume. We should focus on body language: Show them how posture, gestures, and eye contact convey confidence, even when they feel nervous. And we should develop pacing and tone: Teach learners to vary their tone, emphasise key points, and pause for effect to keep their audience engaged.

PROVIDE OPPORTUNITIES FOR LOW-STAKES PRACTICE

Speaking in front of others can be intimidating, so start small. Therefore, we should begin with short, informal discussions in pairs or small groups to reduce the pressure while building confidence, then we should introduce low-stakes activities, such as "60-second speeches" where learners talk about a familiar topic for one minute.

Next, we should ask learners to explain something they're passionate about or narrate a personal story. Familiarity breeds confidence. Once learners feel comfortable with informal speaking, introduce more structured and formal activities such as role-playing scenarios whereby we create real-world situations, such as interviews, debates, or customer interactions, to help learners practise adapting their speech to different contexts. Finally, we should encourage learners to give presentations. Here, we might start with short, informal presentations and gradually increase the length and formality as their confidence grows. We can help by providing clear success criteria, such as organising ideas logically and engaging the audience. Debates and discussions are also key. Here, we should teach learners to articulate and defend their opinions, listen to opposing viewpoints, and respond respectfully. These activities build confidence in thinking on their feet.

USE SENTENCE STEMS AND FRAMEWORKS

For learners who struggle to find the right words, provide scaffolding to help them organise their thoughts. Sentence stems are helpful. These include prompts such as "In my opinion . . .", "One example of this is . . .", or "To summarise my point, I think . . .". Structured frameworks can also prove effective. For example, we could teach frameworks like PEEL (Point, Evidence, Explanation, Link) for structuring their ideas in formal contexts. These tools reduce cognitive load and allow learners to focus on delivery rather than content.

ENCOURAGE REFLECTION AND FEEDBACK

Reflection is key to improvement. We should, therefore, help learners analyse their performance and set goals for future speaking tasks. This might take the form of self-assessment whereby we ask learners to identify what they did well and what they could improve after each speaking task. Or it might take the form of peer feedback whereby we use structured feedback forms to ensure peers provide constructive, actionable advice. Another method is video recording whereby, if appropriate, we record learners' presentations and review the footage together, focusing on strengths and areas for development.

NORMALISE AND REFRAME NERVOUSNESS

Many learners view nervousness as a sign of failure, but it's a natural part of speaking in public. To help, we can teach positive self-talk whereby we encourage learners to replace thoughts like "I'll make a mistake" with "I've prepared well, and I'll do my best". We can also reframe nerves as excitement by explaining that adrenaline is a sign their body is preparing to perform well. And we can help learners practise relaxation techniques such as breathing exercises and visualisation which can help learners manage anxiety before speaking.

EXPOSE LEARNERS TO REAL-WORLD MODELS

Another way to build confidence is to show learners examples of confident speakers in action. We could watch speeches and presentations in class and analyse how successful speakers use body language, tone, and structure to engage their audience. We could invite guest speakers into school to share their experiences and demonstrate the value of confident communication.

Ultimately, speaking confidently is about real-world readiness and so we should try to provide opportunities for learners to use their skills beyond the classroom. We might, for example, encourage learners to take on roles such as head learner or club leader, where they'll need to communicate with confidence. We might involve learners in activities like public readings, assemblies, or outreach projects. And we might simulate job interviews to help learners practise formal speaking in a professional context.

Debating

Talking of confidence, debating is a powerful way to develop learners' self-esteem and oracy skills because it requires them to think critically, express their ideas clearly and confidently, and respond thoughtfully to opposing viewpoints. For disadvantaged learners, debating can also provide an invaluable opportunity to level the playing field, equipping them with the confidence, eloquence, and critical thinking skills often associated with more privileged backgrounds. What's more, debating fosters the ability to argue persuasively, a skill that society frequently mistakes for intelligence and competence. By teaching learners to debate effectively, we not only help them succeed in school but also prepare them to assert themselves in the wider world.

Here's how we might do it . . .

START WITH THE BASICS

Begin by introducing learners to the core principles of debating:

- Structure: Teach the key components of a debate – opening statements, rebuttals, and closing arguments

- Roles: Explain the roles of proposition and opposition teams, as well as the responsibilities of each speaker

- Rules: Establish clear rules for timing, turn-taking, and respectful interaction

Use simple topics initially, such as "Should school uniforms be mandatory?" to help learners focus on the format without being overwhelmed by content.

SCAFFOLD THE SKILLS

Debating is a complex skill, so break it down into manageable steps:

- Teach persuasive techniques: Show learners how to use rhetorical devices, such as anecdotes, statistics, and emotive language, to strengthen their arguments
- Practise rebuttals: Help learners anticipate counterarguments and practise responding confidently, using phrases like "That's a valid point, but . . ."
- Focus on delivery: Encourage learners to speak with appropriate tone, pace, and volume, modelling these behaviours yourself

USE SPEAKING FRAMES AND SENTENCE STARTERS

Support learners who may lack confidence or experience by providing sentence starters, such as:

- "I believe this because . . ."
- "An example of this is . . ."
- "My opponent argues that . . ., but I would counter by saying . . ."

These frames give learners the language to express themselves clearly and help them structure their contributions.

CREATE A SAFE AND SUPPORTIVE ENVIRONMENT

Disadvantaged learners may be more hesitant to participate in debates, so it's vital to create a classroom culture where all voices are valued.

- Start small: Use low-stakes activities, such as pair or small-group debates, before moving to whole-class discussions
- Celebrate effort: Praise learners for participating, even if their arguments are imperfect, to build their confidence
- Provide feedback: Offer constructive feedback on both content and delivery, focusing on strengths and areas for improvement

PRACTISE ACTIVE LISTENING

Effective debating is as much about listening as it is about speaking. Teach learners to:

- Paraphrase opposing arguments: Show understanding by summarising the other side's point before responding

- Ask clarifying questions: Encourage learners to seek more information if an argument is unclear

- Respond respectfully: Model how to challenge ideas without attacking the person presenting them

USE REAL-WORLD CONTEXTS

Choose debate topics that are relevant and meaningful to learners' lives, such as environmental issues, social justice, or school policies. This not only engages them but also helps them see the real-world value of debating skills.

INCORPORATE COMPETITIONS AND PEER FEEDBACK

Once learners are comfortable with the basics, introduce more formal debates and opportunities for peer evaluation. Competitions – whether within the classroom or against other schools – can motivate learners and give them a sense of accomplishment.

Self-evaluation

Here are five self-evaluation questions to consider before you move on:

1. What are the key strategies for creating a safe and supportive environment that fosters confidence in speaking and debating?

2. How can I incorporate low-stakes practice activities into my teaching to help learners build confidence before engaging in formal debates?

3. What specific techniques or tools (e.g., sentence stems, PEEL framework) can I use to scaffold learners' speaking and debating skills effectively?

4. How can I ensure that all learners, particularly those who are disadvantaged or hesitant to participate, feel valued and supported during debates?

5. How can I select debate topics that are both meaningful to learners and encourage critical thinking and engagement with real-world issues?

3. Teach rhetoric and prosody to enable learners to speak convincingly and powerfully to argue their views

Teaching learners to explain their thinking is a crucial element of effective learning. It not only helps them articulate their ideas but also deepens their understanding of the subject matter. When learners can explain their reasoning clearly and confidently, they demonstrate mastery, uncover misconceptions, and lay the groundwork for future learning. But how can we, as educators, support them in this journey?

Here are some practical strategies to help learners explain their thinking with increasing confidence and depth.

ESTABLISH A CLASSROOM CULTURE OF EXPLORATION

To explain their thinking, learners need to feel safe making mistakes and sharing incomplete ideas.

- Normalise struggle: Emphasise that learning is a process of trial and error. Highlight how wrong answers and half-formed ideas are stepping stones to understanding.
- Celebrate curiosity: Praise learners for asking questions and seeking clarity. A curious classroom is one where ideas are explored, not simply stated.
- Encourage respectful dialogue: Foster an environment where learners listen to each other's ideas and respond constructively.

MODEL THINKING ALOUD

Before learners can explain their thinking, they need to see what effective explanation looks like.

- Think aloud as a teacher: Demonstrate your reasoning by verbalising your thought process as you solve problems, make decisions, or evaluate answers. For instance, "I think this works because . . . but I'm not sure about this part yet".
- Highlight metacognition: Explicitly discuss how and why you're choosing certain steps or considering alternative approaches

SCAFFOLD EXPLANATIONS WITH SENTENCE STEMS AND STRUCTURES

Many learners struggle to articulate their thinking because they lack the language to do so. Provide them with tools to structure their responses.

- Sentence stems: Use prompts like: "I think this because . . .", "One example of this is . . .", and "This connects to . . . because . . ."
- Frameworks for depth: Teach structures such as PEEL (Point, Evidence, Explanation, Link) to guide learners in elaborating on their answers

BUILD CONFIDENCE THROUGH LOW-STAKES PRACTICE

Explaining one's thinking can feel intimidating, so begin with activities that allow learners to practise in a low-pressure environment.

- Pair and group discussions: Start with small group work where learners can practise explaining their ideas informally before sharing with the whole class
- Think-Pair-Share: Encourage learners to think individually, then discuss with a partner before sharing their explanations with the class. This gives them time to organise their thoughts.
- Talk tokens: Use tools like 'talk tokens' or discussion cards to ensure every learner contributes in a manageable way

DEEPEN UNDERSTANDING WITH PROBING QUESTIONS

Probing questions encourage learners to reflect on and refine their thinking, moving beyond surface-level responses.

- Ask "why" and "how" questions: Push learners to justify their answers and explain the reasoning behind their conclusions. For example, "Why do you think that?" or "How did you arrive at that conclusion?"
- Encourage connections: Prompt learners to relate their ideas to prior knowledge or other concepts. For example, "How does this link to what we learned last lesson?"
- Challenge assumptions: Ask questions that prompt learners to consider alternative perspectives or solutions. For example, "What if we approached this differently?"

USE VISUAL TOOLS TO SUPPORT THINKING

Some learners find it easier to explain their thinking when they can visualise their ideas.

- Mind maps and diagrams: Encourage learners to organise their thoughts visually before explaining them
- Think boards: Provide structured templates where learners can jot down key points, evidence, and connections before verbalising their explanations

ENCOURAGE PEER EXPLANATION

Explaining to others is one of the most effective ways to deepen understanding.

- Teach-back activities: Ask learners to teach a concept to a peer or small group. This requires them to articulate their ideas clearly and think about the best way to explain them.
- Peer critique: Have learners explain their reasoning to a partner and receive constructive feedback on the clarity and depth of their explanation

EMBED OPPORTUNITIES FOR REFLECTION

Reflection helps learners identify strengths and areas for improvement in their explanations.

- Self-assessment: Provide checklists or rubrics so learners can evaluate their own explanations. For example, "Did I justify my answer?", "Did I provide examples or evidence?", and "Did I link my ideas to prior learning?"
- Peer feedback: Encourage learners to review each other's explanations and suggest ways to add depth or clarity
- Class discussions: Reflect as a group on what makes an effective explanation, using examples from learners' own work

GRADUALLY INCREASE THE CHALLENGE

As learners grow more confident, push them to explain their thinking in more complex and challenging contexts.

- Introduce unfamiliar problems: Present scenarios where learners need to apply their knowledge in new ways, requiring deeper explanation
- Incorporate open-ended tasks: Use questions with no single correct answer, encouraging learners to justify their reasoning and explore alternatives
- Ask for counterarguments: Challenge learners to critique their own thinking or consider opposing viewpoints

MAKE THINKING VISIBLE IN WRITING AND SPEECH

Encourage learners to explain their thinking not just verbally but also in writing. Writing allows them to organise and deepen their ideas before sharing aloud.

- Think-Write-Share: Have learners write their explanation first, then share it with the class
- Annotation: Ask learners to annotate their work with notes explaining the decisions they made and why
- Double-response tasks: Require learners to provide both a written and verbal explanation of their reasoning, reinforcing their understanding

We'll explore rhetoric in a moment, but first let's talk about spoken language capability . . .

Spoken language

The ability to use spoken language effectively is a cornerstone of success in school and beyond. Strong oracy skills not only support academic achievement but also foster confidence, critical thinking, and social engagement. Developing children's spoken language capability requires intentional teaching and a classroom culture that values talk. Here are some practical strategies that educators can use to unlock every child's verbal potential.

Here are some suggestions for developing learners' spoken language capability:

PRIORITISE TALK IN THE CLASSROOM

If we want children to develop their spoken language skills, we must create regular and meaningful opportunities for them to talk.

- Use structured talk tasks: Incorporate activities like debates, role-plays, and group discussions into lessons. Assign clear roles to ensure all learners contribute.
- Think-Pair-Share: After posing a question, give learners time to think individually, then discuss their ideas with a partner before sharing with the class. This scaffolds confidence and ensures all voices are heard.
- Exploratory talk: Encourage learners to talk through ideas without fear of getting it "wrong". Use prompts such as, "What do you think might happen if . . .?" or "Why do you think that is the case?"

TEACH THE ART OF LISTENING

Speaking well begins with listening well. Children need to learn how to actively engage with what others are saying.

- Model active listening: Show learners how to listen attentively by making eye contact, nodding, and responding thoughtfully
- Teach summarising skills: After a peer speaks, ask learners to paraphrase what they've heard before adding their own thoughts. For example, "I agree with Samira because . . ." or "I see it differently because . . .".
- Use listening challenges: Set tasks that require learners to listen carefully, such as following multi-step instructions or answering questions based on a peer's explanation

BUILD VOCABULARY EXPLICITLY

A strong vocabulary is the foundation of articulacy. Children need the words to express themselves clearly and precisely.

- Word of the day: Introduce a new word each day, model its use in context, and encourage learners to incorporate it into their speech

- Subject-specific language: Teach the key vocabulary of each subject and provide opportunities to use it in discussions
- Play word games: Use games like "Taboo" or "Word Association" to make vocabulary development engaging and fun

SCAFFOLD SPOKEN RESPONSES

Many children struggle to articulate their thoughts because they don't know how to structure their speech. Provide scaffolds to support them.

- Sentence stems: Offer prompts such as: "I think this because . . .", "One example of this is . . .", and "This connects to . . . because . . .".
- Talk frameworks: Teach learners how to organise their ideas using structures like PEEL (Point, Evidence, Explanation, Link) for discussions
- Rehearse answers: Allow learners to rehearse their responses in pairs or small groups before sharing with the class

ENCOURAGE FORMAL AND INFORMAL TALK

Children need to practise speaking in a variety of contexts, from casual conversations to formal presentations.

- Casual talk zones: Create spaces in the classroom where learners can engage in informal discussions, such as a "debate corner" or a "question wall"
- Presentations and performances: Build learners' confidence by giving them opportunities to present to the class, perform in plays, or lead assemblies
- Mock interviews: Practise formal communication through role-play scenarios like job interviews or news reporting

FOSTER A CULTURE OF TALK

A classroom culture that values talk encourages learners to take risks and develop their verbal skills.

- Celebrate talk: Praise learners for thoughtful contributions and effective communication, not just correct answers
- Talk rules: Co-create rules for effective discussions, such as taking turns, respecting others' opinions, and backing up ideas with evidence
- Showcase talk: Invite guest speakers or organise debate competitions to demonstrate the power of spoken language

USE TECHNOLOGY TO ENHANCE ORACY

Technology can provide innovative ways to develop spoken language skills.

- Record and review: Use audio or video recordings to help learners reflect on their speech and identify areas for improvement
- Digital storytelling: Encourage learners to create and narrate their own multimedia projects
- Speech apps: Use apps that provide feedback on pronunciation, fluency, or pace to help learners refine their skills

INTEGRATE TALK ACROSS THE CURRICULUM

Spoken language development shouldn't be confined to English lessons. Embed oracy into every subject.

- Talk for maths reasoning: Ask learners to explain their problem-solving steps or justify their answers
- Science discussions: Use group talk to plan experiments, interpret data, or debate ethical issues
- History role-plays: Bring the past to life by having learners debate historical decisions in character

PROVIDE TARGETED SUPPORT

Some learners may need additional help to develop their spoken language capability.

- Small group interventions: Work with learners in small groups to build confidence and practise foundational skills
- Oracy mentors: Pair less confident learners with peers who can model effective communication
- Speech and language therapy: Collaborate with specialists to support learners with specific needs

CELEBRATE PROGRESS

Encourage learners to see themselves as capable speakers by celebrating their growth.

- Oracy portfolios: Keep a record of learners' speeches, presentations, and discussions to show how their skills have improved over time

- Class showcases: Organise events where learners can demonstrate their oracy skills, such as poetry recitals or public speaking competitions
- Reflect on achievements: Use self-assessment and peer feedback to help learners recognise their progress and set goals for further development

Rhetoric

Rhetoric – the art of persuasion – is a powerful tool that allows individuals to articulate their ideas, influence others, and navigate the world with confidence. For disadvantaged learners, learning rhetoric is not merely about mastering a skill; it is about levelling the playing field. It equips them with the ability to compete with their more affluent peers, who often gain these skills through osmosis in language-rich, opportunity-filled environments.

Teaching rhetoric should not be seen as a luxury but as a necessity, an essential component of education that enables disadvantaged learners to find their voice and assert their place in the world. Here's how schools can ensure all learners, regardless of background, master the art of rhetoric:

BUILD A FOUNDATION OF ORACY

Effective rhetoric begins with strong oracy skills. Learners need to feel confident in their ability to speak and be heard before they can craft persuasive arguments. In practice, we might therefore:

- Encourage exploratory talk: Use activities such as debates, role-plays, and Socratic discussions to create a safe environment where learners can practise expressing their ideas
- Develop listening skills: Teach learners to listen actively, identify key points, and respond thoughtfully to others' arguments
- Use sentence stems: Provide scaffolds like "I agree with . . . because . . ." or "My perspective differs because . . ." to help learners structure their responses

TEACH THE ELEMENTS OF RHETORIC

Aristotle's three modes of persuasion – ethos, pathos, and logos – remain the cornerstones of compelling arguments. We should therefore explicitly teach these elements and how to use them effectively:

- Ethos (credibility): Show learners how to establish trust and authority by citing reliable evidence and demonstrating knowledge

- Pathos (emotion): Teach learners to connect with their audience emotionally by using anecdotes, vivid imagery, and empathy
- Logos (logic): Help learners construct logical arguments using facts, statistics, and clear reasoning

PROVIDE EXPLICIT INSTRUCTION IN ARGUMENTATION

Disadvantaged learners may not naturally encounter environments where formal argumentation is modelled or practised. Schools must fill this gap with direct teaching. We can do this by:

- Breaking down the structure: Teach the components of a strong argument – introduction, thesis, supporting points, counterarguments, and conclusion
- Modelling good practice: Show examples of effective speeches and essays, analysing what makes them compelling
- Rehearsing and refining: Use peer feedback and multiple drafts to help learners polish their arguments

USE RHETORICAL DEVICES

We can teach learners how to employ rhetorical techniques to make their arguments memorable and persuasive, including:

- Alliteration and repetition: Demonstrate how these can emphasise key points and make speeches more engaging
- Rhetorical questions: Encourage learners to ask thought-provoking questions that challenge their audience's assumptions
- Contrast and juxtaposition: Show how comparing opposing ideas can strengthen their case

EMBED RHETORIC ACROSS THE CURRICULUM AND BEYOND

The art of persuasion should not be confined to English lessons. We should embed opportunities for rhetorical practice in every subject. Here are some examples:

- History: Debate historical decisions, imagining the perspectives of key figures
- Science: Ask learners to argue for or against controversial issues such as genetic modification or climate policies
- PSHE: Use role-play to discuss ethical dilemmas and practise persuasive speaking

Nor should rhetoric be confined to the school curriculum. Rather, for rhetoric to feel relevant, learners need opportunities to apply it in authentic contexts. Here are some examples:

- Run mock trials: Allow learners to argue cases, practising constructing and defending their positions

- Organise debates: Host inter-class or inter-school debate competitions to showcase learners' rhetorical skills

- Engage with the community: Involve learners in presenting ideas to local councils, businesses, or charities, giving their arguments a practical purpose

Teaching rhetoric is about far more than honing speaking skills; it is about empowering disadvantaged learners to find their voice and take their place in the world. By providing explicit instruction, real-world practice, and opportunities to succeed, schools can help every child – regardless of background – master the art of persuasion. In doing so, we equip them with the tools to challenge inequality, shape their futures, and thrive in a society that values confident, articulate voices.

Prosody

Another element of helping learners to speak convincingly and powerfully to argue their views is prosody – which is to say, the ability to speak articulately – with clarity, confidence, and appropriate tone, pace, and tempo. Prosody enables learners to express their ideas effectively, connect with diverse audiences, and succeed in academic, social, and professional contexts. However, many young people, particularly those from disadvantaged backgrounds, may lack opportunities to develop these skills naturally.

We can bridge this gap by explicitly teaching the mechanics of articulate speech. By embedding these skills into everyday practice and creating safe spaces for rehearsal, educators can help every learner find their voice and use it to maximum effect. Here's how:

MODEL EFFECTIVE SPEECH

Learners learn best when they see and hear high-quality examples of articulate speech. As such, we can:

- Showcase role models: Use speeches, debates, and interviews by respected speakers to demonstrate effective communication

- Demonstrate in the classroom: Teachers should model clear, confident speech, varying tone, pace, and tempo to suit the context

- Use peer examples: Encourage learners to identify and emulate strong speakers among their peers, fostering a culture of mutual inspiration

TEACH THE FUNDAMENTALS OF ARTICULATION

Articulate speech relies on mastery of tone, pace, and tempo. These can be broken down into the following teachable components:

- Tone: Explain how tone conveys emotion and intent. Use activities like reading aloud in different tones (e.g., persuasive, empathetic, authoritative) to help learners experiment with vocal variation.
- Pace: Teach learners to adjust their speaking speed to maintain audience engagement. Practise pacing with timed activities, such as delivering a one-minute explanation or pausing deliberately between points.
- Tempo: Highlight how the rhythm of speech adds emphasis and clarity. Use clapping or tapping exercises to help learners understand natural pauses and sentence flow.

EMBED PRACTICE IN EVERYDAY LESSONS

Speaking articulately should not be an occasional activity but a regular feature of classroom life. For example, we could:

- Encourage verbal explanations: Ask learners to articulate their reasoning aloud, using full sentences and precise vocabulary
- Use questioning techniques: Pose open-ended questions that require thoughtful, detailed responses. Follow up with prompts like, "Can you expand on that?"
- Facilitate discussions: Organise structured discussions where learners practise speaking to different audiences, from peers to the whole class.

USE SCAFFOLDS AND SUPPORTS

For learners to speak articulately, they need tools to structure their thoughts and build confidence. To help, we might:

- Provide sentence stems: Offer phrases like "I believe this because . . ." or "In conclusion, I would argue that . . ." to help learners organise their ideas
- Teach rhetorical devices: Show learners how repetition, contrast, and rhetorical questions can make their speech more engaging
- Use visual aids: Provide mind maps or key word prompts to help learners stay on track during verbal explanations

REHEARSE PUBLIC SPEAKING

Public speaking is a powerful way to develop tone, pace, and tempo. We should, therefore, create opportunities for learners to practise in a supportive environment. We might do this by:

- Running speaking workshops: Teach techniques for breath control, projection, and clear enunciation
- Hosting presentations: Encourage learners to present their work to the class, focusing on delivery as well as content
- Organising debates: Use debates to help learners practise persuasive tone, logical pacing, and confident tempo under time constraints

CREATE SAFE SPACES FOR SPEAKING

Building confidence is as important as teaching technique. To help, we might:

- Start small: Begin with low-stakes activities, such as partner discussions, before progressing to larger audiences
- Celebrate progress: Acknowledge each learner's improvements, no matter how incremental, to boost confidence
- Normalise mistakes: Emphasise that missteps are part of learning, encouraging learners to take risks and try again

We might also reinforce the importance of listening by:

- Modelling active listening: Show learners how to engage with speakers by making eye contact, nodding, and asking questions
- Practising turn-taking: Use activities that require learners to listen carefully and build on others' ideas
- Encouraging reflective responses: Teach learners to paraphrase or summarise what they've heard before contributing their own thoughts

Self-evaluation

Here are five self-evaluation questions to consider before you move on:

1. How effectively do I foster a classroom environment that encourages exploration and open dialogue among learners? Reflect on whether your classroom promotes curiosity, respectful dialogue, and a safe space for sharing incomplete ideas.

2. Do I model and scaffold effective verbal and written explanations for my learners? Consider whether you regularly demonstrate thinking aloud, use sentence stems, and provide structured frameworks like PEEL.

3. How well do I integrate spoken language development into various aspects of the curriculum? Evaluate whether you provide opportunities for learners to articulate their thinking across subjects and in diverse formats, such as debates and presentations.

4. Am I equipping my learners with the skills to use rhetorical techniques and prosody effectively in their speech? Think about how you teach elements like ethos, pathos, and logos, as well as tone, pace, and tempo in speech delivery.

5. Do I provide sufficient opportunities for learners to practice and refine their communication skills in low-stakes and high-stakes settings? Reflect on the balance between informal practice activities, such as pair discussions, and more formal settings like presentations or debates.

4. Teach storytelling techniques to enable learners to narrate their own lives and the lives of others

Storytelling lies at the heart of human communication. From ancient oral traditions to modern narratives, it is how we share knowledge, connect with others, and make sense of the world. For learners, storytelling is not just a creative pursuit; it is a powerful means of developing oracy skills, equipping them to express themselves with clarity, confidence, and purpose.

Why? Because when learners learn to craft and deliver stories, they sharpen their ability to structure thoughts, engage listeners, and adapt their speech for different audiences. They gain tools to articulate their ideas, explain their thinking, and persuade others, all while nurturing empathy and imagination. In short, storytelling is a gateway to richer communication, deeper understanding, and greater self-expression.

Here's why storytelling matters and how we can teach it effectively.

Storytelling teaches learners to organise their thoughts logically. The narrative arc – beginning, middle, and end – helps them construct coherent responses, whether recounting events or building arguments.

Crafting stories encourages learners to experiment with language, selecting words and phrases to evoke emotion, create imagery, or convey meaning effectively.

Sharing stories in a supportive environment helps learners gain confidence in public speaking while fostering creativity and self-expression.

Storytelling requires learners to consider their audience, adapting tone, pace, and detail to hold attention and make an impact.

Through stories, learners explore perspectives beyond their own, fostering understanding and emotional intelligence.

Teaching storytelling is about breaking the process into manageable steps, providing structure, and creating opportunities for practice and feedback. Accordingly, we might:

INTRODUCE THE ELEMENTS OF A GOOD STORY

We might help learners understand what makes a story compelling by focusing on key elements:

- Characters: Encourage learners to create relatable, multidimensional characters. Use role-play to bring characters to life and explore their motivations.
- Setting: Teach learners to establish a vivid sense of place. Use sensory language – what can be seen, heard, or felt?
- Conflict: Highlight the importance of a problem or challenge to drive the narrative. Ask learners to brainstorm conflicts that engage the audience.
- Resolution: Discuss how stories resolve, leaving the audience with a sense of closure or a thought-provoking twist.

TEACH NARRATIVE STRUCTURE

We might introduce learners to the classic narrative arc:

- Exposition: Set the scene and introduce the characters
- Rising action: Build tension with challenges or conflicts
- Climax: Reach the turning point or moment of greatest tension
- Falling action: Show the consequences of the climax
- Resolution: Tie up loose ends or deliver a final message

PRACTISE VERBAL STORYTELLING SKILLS

Effective storytelling relies on more than words; delivery matters. As such, we might focus on:

- Tone and emotion: Model how to use tone to reflect the mood of the story. Practise by retelling the same story in different emotional tones.
- Pace and pauses: Teach learners to vary their speaking speed and use pauses for dramatic effect. Practise this with short anecdotes.
- Gestures and expressions: Encourage learners to use body language and facial expressions to enhance their stories.

- Audience engagement: Help learners develop techniques like making eye contact, asking rhetorical questions, or inviting participation.

USE SCAFFOLDING AND STORY PROMPTS

Some learners may feel intimidated by open-ended storytelling tasks. Accordingly, we might provide scaffolds to help them get started, such as:

- Sentence starters: Offer phrases like "Once upon a time . . ." or "The problem began when . . ." to guide learners
- Story maps: Use graphic organisers to help learners plan their narratives, identifying key events and transitions
- Story cubes or cards: Provide prompts featuring characters, settings, and conflicts to inspire creativity

INCORPORATE STORYTELLING ACROSS THE CURRICULUM

Storytelling is not confined to English lessons; it can enrich learning in all subjects. For example:

- In history, we might encourage learners to retell historical events from the perspective of key figures.
- In science, we might ask learners to narrate the life of a raindrop or the journey of a cell, blending facts with imagination.
- In maths, we might use stories to explain mathematical concepts or create real-world problem-solving scenarios.

Self-evaluation

Here are five self-evaluation questions to consider before you move on:

1. How well do I understand the significance of storytelling as a tool for communication and learning? Can I articulate its benefits for oracy, creativity, and empathy?

2. What techniques or strategies mentioned in this chapter could I apply in my own teaching or learning environment to improve storytelling skills?

3. Which aspects of the storytelling framework (e.g., narrative arc, character development, verbal delivery) resonate most with me, and why? Are there any I find less convincing or applicable?

4. Have I observed or experienced situations where storytelling enhanced understanding or engagement? How might this chapter influence the way I approach storytelling in the future?

5. Can I think of creative ways to incorporate storytelling techniques into subjects or contexts beyond language arts, as suggested by the examples in this chapter?

5. Deploy dialogic teaching and modelling in the classroom to make oracy an integral part of the curriculum

Dialogic teaching – an approach that places purposeful dialogue at the heart of learning – can play a crucial role in helping learners develop the skills they need to speak with clarity, confidence, and precision.

Oracy is not simply about learning to talk; it is about learning through talk. Dialogic teaching amplifies this principle, providing a structured framework in which learners can sharpen their verbal communication, deepen their understanding, and build the confidence to express themselves effectively in diverse contexts.

At its core, dialogic teaching is about creating a classroom culture where dialogue drives learning. It involves more than surface-level exchanges; it is characterised by:

- Cumulative talk, where learners build on each other's contributions to develop shared understanding
- Exploratory talk, where they test and refine ideas through discussion
- Reflective talk, where they evaluate their own and others' perspectives

This approach shifts the focus from teacher-led instruction to a co-constructed learning experience, where learners play an active role in their own and others' intellectual development.

Dialogic teaching supports the development of learners' oracy skills in several ways, including by:

Encouraging clarity and coherence – through guided discussions, learners learn to organise their thoughts, express ideas logically, and articulate their reasoning with greater clarity.

Building confidence and fluency – regular opportunities to speak in a supportive environment help learners gain confidence and improve the fluency of their speech.

Fostering active listening – dialogic teaching emphasises listening as much as speaking, helping learners develop the ability to engage thoughtfully with others' ideas.

Expanding vocabulary and language structures – exposure to rich, varied dialogue enables learners to adopt new words and phrases, enhancing their verbal repertoire.

Promoting adaptability – by engaging with diverse perspectives, learners learn to adjust their tone, language, and approach to suit different audiences and purposes.

To harness the full potential of dialogic teaching for oracy development, we might employ the following strategies:

ESTABLISH GROUND RULES FOR DIALOGUE

We might seek to create a classroom culture where learners feel comfortable contributing and where talk is purposeful and respectful. We can do this by:

- Agreeing on norms: Work with learners to establish rules for listening, turn-taking, and challenging ideas constructively
- Modelling effective dialogue: Demonstrate how to build on others' ideas, ask thoughtful questions, and disagree respectfully

USE OPEN-ENDED QUESTIONS

We might stimulate rich, meaningful discussions by asking questions that encourage learners to think deeply and articulate their reasoning. We can do this by:

- Posing thought-provoking prompts: Use questions like "Why do you think that?" or "What evidence supports your view?" to elicit detailed responses.
- Encouraging multiple perspectives: Ask, "Does anyone have a different opinion?" to invite diverse contributions.

FACILITATE STRUCTURED DISCUSSIONS

We might provide frameworks that guide learners to engage in productive dialogue. These include:

- Think-pair-share: Allow learners time to formulate their thoughts individually before discussing them with a partner and then sharing with the class
- Debates: Organise debates on relevant topics, teaching learners to construct arguments, use persuasive techniques, and respond to counterpoints
- Socratic seminars: Use open-ended questions to facilitate learner-led discussions on complex issues, encouraging deep exploration of ideas

TEACH 'TALK MOVES'

We might equip learners with verbal tools that help them participate effectively in dialogue, such as:

- Revoicing: Encourage learners to paraphrase or clarify others' ideas to ensure understanding

- Building on: Teach them to extend or add to a peer's contribution, saying, "I'd like to add to that . . ."

- Probing: Show them how to ask follow-up questions, such as "Can you explain why?"

Modelling oracy

Of course, dialogic teaching is not just about developing oracy skills; it also enhances learners' cognitive, social, and emotional growth. It encourages critical thinking, nurtures empathy, and builds collaborative problem-solving skills. For disadvantaged learners, in particular, it can be transformative, providing opportunities to practise articulating their ideas and building the confidence to assert themselves in the world.

As well as dialogic teaching, we need to model good oracy if we are to help learners develop these skills. After all, learners learn as much from what they observe as from what they are taught, and when teachers consistently demonstrate good oracy, we provide a living example of what articulate, confident, and purposeful speech looks like.

Modelling good oracy is not about delivering polished speeches or adopting an unnatural formality; it is about showing learners how to use language effectively to express ideas, engage listeners, and build understanding. It requires intentionality and a focus on the nuances of spoken communication – tone, pace, clarity, and the ability to adapt to different audiences.

Modelling oracy is about setting the standard. By modelling good oracy, teachers establish high expectations for communication, showing learners the skills and behaviours they should emulate.

It's also about building a culture of communication because modelling oracy fosters a classroom environment where speaking and listening are valued and practised as essential tools for learning and collaboration.

In practice, this means we must demonstrate clear and confident speaking. We can do this by:

- Articulating our ideas clearly: Speak in full sentences, use precise language, and avoid filler words like "um" or "you know". This demonstrates clarity of thought and purpose.

- Varying our tone and pace: Show how tone can convey emotion or intent, and use pace to emphasise key points. For example, slow down for complex ideas and pause to let important messages resonate.

- Projecting our voice: You should speak with appropriate volume and energy, ensuring you are easily heard while modelling confidence and authority.

We can also choose our words carefully and thus model the use of subject-specific vocabulary and encourage learners to adopt these terms in their own speech. We can rephrase for clarity to show learners how to adjust language for different audiences, offering simpler explanations when necessary, without diluting meaning. And we can encourage verbal variety by using synonyms and descriptive language to bring ideas to life and avoid repetition.

A further strategy for modelling good oracy is to ask thoughtful questions. In particular, we could use open-ended prompts and ask questions like "What do you think about . . .?" or "Why might this be the case?" to invite detailed responses. We could probe for depth and follow up with "Can you explain further?" or "What makes you say that?" to encourage deeper thinking and more articulate answers. And we can balance contributions by modelling inclusive questioning by ensuring all learners have the chance to speak, showing the importance of valuing every voice.

As well as modelling speaking, we must model active listening. For example, we can model making eye contact and thus show attentiveness by looking at the speaker, nodding, or using encouraging expressions. We can model the use of paraphrasing and summarising to reflect back what learners have said, e.g., "So you're saying that . . ." or "In other words . . .". This demonstrates understanding and respect for their contributions. And we can respond constructively by building on learners' ideas with phrases like "That's an interesting point. Let's explore it further . . .".

Thinking aloud is crucial, too, because learners need to see 'our workings', they need to see the process not just the product. Modelling our thought processes helps learners understand how to structure and articulate their own reasoning. For this, we could verbalise our approach to solving problems, e.g., "I'm considering both sides of the argument because . . .". We could explain our choices. For example, when presenting information, we could highlight why certain words or tones are effective, e.g., "I'm using this example to help clarify my point". And we could demonstrate reflection by showing how we evaluate our own ideas, saying, "I might revise that because . . .".

We talked earlier about code-switching and it's important for teachers to model how we adjust our communication style depending on the situation. To do this, we might switch between formal and informal tones, using conversational language in small group discussions but adopting a more formal tone during whole-class instruction, presentations or assemblies. We might adjust our vocabulary according to context, too. For example, when introducing complex concepts, we might model how to simplify explanations without losing meaning. And we might tailor our language to connect with different audiences, demonstrating sensitivity to their needs and perspectives.

As well as modelling good oracy, we can make use of speaking frames and rules. Oracy is not an innate talent but a skill that can be taught, practised, and refined. To help learners become confident and articulate communicators, we need to provide structured support that builds learners' capabilities incrementally. Two powerful tools in this process are speaking frames and rule-setting. Together, these strategies create a safe, scaffolded environment where learners can experiment with language, practise essential skills, and develop their voices.

Speaking frames are sentence structures or prompts that guide learners in constructing their responses. They act as a bridge, supporting learners to move from hesitant, fragmented speech to fluent, confident articulation.

Speaking frames might provide a starting point for learners' talk. After all, many learners struggle to speak because they don't know how to begin but speaking frames remove this barrier by offering a clear opening and a logical structure. Speaking frames can also help learners express their ideas fully, avoiding one-word answers or incomplete thoughts.

Speaking frames might also help build confidence because they reduce cognitive load and thus allow learners to focus on their ideas rather than worrying about how to phrase them.

And speaking frames can be used to introduce subject-specific vocabulary and complex sentence structures, thus helping learners speak with greater precision and sophistication.

Speaking frames can be tailored to different purposes, from explaining concepts to debating ideas. For example:

Explaining:

- "I think this because . . ."
- "The evidence for this is . . ."
- "An example of this is . . ."

Building on ideas:

- "I agree with [name] because . . ."
- "To add to what [name] said . . ."

Disagreeing respectfully:

- "I see your point, but I think . . ."
- "Another perspective might be . . ."

Making predictions:

- "I predict that . . . because . . ."
- "This might happen because . . ."

Reflecting:

- "I learned that . . ."
- "One thing I found challenging was . . ."

Rule-setting establishes the expectations and behaviours that underpin effective dialogue. When learners know how to interact respectfully and purposefully, they feel more confident participating in discussions. Clear rules ensure every learner has the opportunity to contribute, fostering a sense of belonging and confidence. Rules emphasise the importance of listening as well as speaking, helping learners engage thoughtfully with others' ideas. By setting expectations for how to disagree constructively and take turns, rules create a safe environment for open dialogue. When learners understand the ground rules, they are more likely to take responsibility for the quality of their contributions.

Here are some examples of rules we might use for oracy:

Respectful listening

- "Listen carefully to the speaker without interrupting."
- "Show you are listening through eye contact and positive body language."

Constructive dialogue

- "Build on what others say rather than dismissing their ideas."
- "Challenge ideas, not people."

Participation

- "Ensure everyone has a chance to speak before speaking again yourself."
- "Encourage quieter members of the group to contribute."

Clarity and focus

- "Speak in full sentences and stay on topic."
- "Use evidence to support your ideas."

The best rules tend to be co-created with learners. Involving learners in defining the ground rules for discussions helps ensure they feel ownership and understand their purpose. Displaying the rules prominently in the classroom and referring to them regularly helps to reinforce expectations.

Self-evaluation

Here are five self-evaluation questions to consider before you move on:

1. How well do I understand the principles and benefits of dialogic teaching for developing oracy skills?

2. Can I identify specific strategies, such as using open-ended questions or facilitating structured discussions, that I could implement in my teaching practice?

3. How effectively do I model good oracy skills, such as clear articulation, active listening, and appropriate tone and language adaptation?

4. Do I make effective use of tools like speaking frames and rule-setting to support and guide learners in developing their verbal communication skills?

5. How successful am I in fostering a classroom environment where dialogue is respectful, purposeful, and inclusive, encouraging learners to participate actively?

It's all about confidence

Oracy is about confident communication, and confidence is the cornerstone of success. Confidence shapes how learners approach challenges, interact with peers, and view their own potential.

For disadvantaged learners, however, confidence is often in short supply, eroded by the barriers of poverty, limited opportunities, and the weight of societal expectations. Schools play a critical role in reversing this narrative, helping learners believe in themselves and their capacity to succeed.

The task is not about simply building self-esteem; it's about fostering resilience, cultivating self-efficacy, and creating a foundation for lifelong confidence.

So, in addition to what I say earlier about oracy, here's how schools can empower disadvantaged learners to thrive.

1. Build strong relationships

Confidence grows when learners feel valued and supported by the adults around them. To help, we can:

- Prioritise trust: Take time to build strong, positive relationships with learners. We should show genuine interest in their lives and aspirations.

- Offer consistency: Ensure learners experience a stable, predictable environment where they feel safe to take risks and express themselves

- Provide encouragement: Praise effort, not just outcomes, and celebrate progress at every step of the journey

2. Set high expectations

Learners gain confidence when they are challenged to achieve and supported to succeed. To help, we can:

- Believe in potential: Show learners that you expect them to excel, regardless of their starting point. We should avoid lowering standards based on assumptions about background or ability.

- Differentiate for success: Provide the scaffolding necessary to ensure all learners can meet ambitious goals

- Celebrate achievement: Recognise and reward accomplishments, however small, to reinforce a growth mindset

3. Teach resilience and a belief in learning from mistakes

Disadvantaged learners may feel defined by failure. Schools can help them reframe challenges as opportunities to learn and grow, including by:

- Normalising setbacks: Share stories of successful individuals who overcame adversity. You should model resilience by reflecting on your own experiences of failure.
- Using language carefully: Focus on effort and perseverance rather than fixed traits, using phrases like "You worked hard to achieve that" or "What can we learn from this?"
- Teaching strategies for self-regulation: Equip learners with tools to manage stress, such as mindfulness techniques or goal-setting frameworks

4. Provide opportunities for success

Confidence grows through experience. Learners need regular opportunities to demonstrate their abilities and take pride in their achievements. To help, we can:

- Create leadership roles: Assign responsibilities that allow learners to contribute meaningfully to the school community, such as mentoring younger peers or leading a project
- Encourage public speaking: Build confidence through activities like class presentations, debates, or assemblies. We should scaffold these tasks to ensure success.
- Support extracurricular involvement: Help learners access clubs, sports, or creative activities where they can develop skills and form positive relationships

5. Develop communication skills

As I've already argued, articulacy is often mistaken for aptitude, yet disadvantaged learners may lack exposure to language-rich environments. Teaching communication skills directly can enhance confidence. For example, we might:

- Practise speaking and listening: Use activities such as group discussions, role-plays, and storytelling to help learners express themselves
- Teach persuasive techniques: Show learners how to construct arguments and present ideas with conviction
- Celebrate all contributions: Ensure every learner feels their voice is heard and valued, regardless of their confidence level

6. Create a culture of belonging

Learners are more confident when they feel they belong and their identity is respected. Such a culture can be created when we:

- Promote inclusivity: Celebrate diversity and challenge stereotypes, creating a school culture where all learners feel valued

- Recognise individuality: Encourage learners to explore their interests and talents, showing that their unique qualities are strengths

- Address barriers: Provide targeted support to help learners overcome challenges, whether financial, emotional, or academic

7. Foster positive peer relationships

Peer dynamics can either build or undermine confidence. Schools must help learners develop supportive, respectful relationships, including by:

- Encouraging collaboration: Use group work to teach teamwork and mutual respect

- Tackling bullying proactively: Take swift, decisive action to address negative behaviours and promote kindness

- Modelling respect: Ensure staff demonstrate the behaviours they wish to see in learners, such as active listening and valuing all opinions

8. Expose learners to new experiences

Disadvantaged learners may have limited access to the experiences that help build confidence in affluent peers. Schools can help bridge this gap by:

- Organising trips and visits: Take learners to museums, universities, workplaces, or cultural events to broaden their horizons

- Bringing the world into school: Invite guest speakers, run workshops, or use virtual reality to introduce learners to new ideas and opportunities

- Encouraging aspiration: Show learners what's possible by exposing them to diverse role models and career paths

9. Involve families

Confidence-building doesn't stop at the school gate, of course. Rather, we must involve families in the process to ensure that learners receive consistent messages of support and encouragement. We might do this by:

- Celebrating achievements together: Share successes with families through newsletters, phone calls, or events
- Providing parental workshops: Help parents and carers support their child's confidence and learning at home
- Building partnerships: Work collaboratively with families to overcome barriers and create a shared vision for success

10. Measure and reflect on progress

Confidence is not built overnight. It takes time and is a war of attrition. Along the way, we need to monitor progress, reflect on successes, and adapt our approaches. To help, we might:

- Encourage learners to reflect on their growth and set personal goals for improvement
- Look for increases in participation, attendance, or willingness to take risks as signs of growing confidence
- Remind learners of how far they've come, reinforcing the belief that they can continue to succeed

Self-esteem

Confidence is not a gift reserved for the fortunate few; it is a skill that can be nurtured in every learner. By creating environments where disadvantaged learners feel valued, supported, and capable, schools can empower them to embrace challenges, achieve their potential, and face the world with self-assurance. Confidence, after all, is not just about self-belief – it is about unlocking opportunity and shaping a brighter future.

So far, we've explored the importance of building learners' confidence in their communications, helping them to articulate their thoughts and engage in debates and discussions. But confidence is also about self-esteem, a belief in your own worth and ability. Without such a belief, learners are unlikely to develop the oracy skills needed to make their own way in the world.

Self-esteem shapes how learners approach challenges, interact with others, and perceive their potential. Yet, for many children, particularly those from disadvantaged backgrounds, low self-esteem can act as a significant barrier to learning and growth.

Schools, as hubs of support and opportunity, are uniquely positioned to help learners develop a positive sense of self. By fostering a culture of inclusion, recognition, and growth, educators can empower every child to see themselves as capable, valued, and worthy of success. Here are some practical suggestions to help learners build self-belief . . .

Learners thrive when they feel recognised for what they do well. Schools can help build self-esteem by acknowledging and celebrating each learner's strengths.

As such, we might recognise individual achievements by praising learners for effort as well as results, ensuring every child has moments of success to celebrate; we might broaden definitions of success by valuing achievements across a range of domains – academic, creative, sporting, or social – so all learners feel their unique contributions are valued; and we might use positive reinforcement by framing feedback constructively, focusing on what learners have done well and how they can build on their strengths.

A fixed mindset, in which learners believe their abilities are set in stone, can undermine self-esteem. Instead, schools should promote a growth mindset – the belief that ability grows with effort. For example, we might normalise the making of mistakes by showing learners that mistakes are a natural part of learning by modelling resilience and celebrating the lessons learned from setbacks. We might use language carefully by emphasising phrases like "not yet" instead of "can't" to reinforce the idea that success is a journey. And we might teach the science of growth by explaining to learners how the brain forms new connections through effort, helping them see that they have the power to improve.

Learners are more likely to feel confident and valued when they belong to a supportive community. This could involve building relationships, ensuring every learner feels known and cared for by fostering strong teacher-learner connections. This could involve celebrating diversity and challenge discrimination, creating a space where all learners feel respected and accepted. And it could involve establishing clear boundaries, creating a well-ordered environment with consistent rules to help learners feel secure and valued.

Giving learners responsibility and ownership can also help them see themselves as capable and influential. We might, for example, assign responsibilities such as leading discussions, mentoring peers, or managing resources. We might encourage learners to participate in decision-making processes and extracurricular activities. And we might highlight how learners' actions, no matter how small, make a positive difference in their school community.

Self-esteem is closely tied to how learners manage emotions and navigate relationships. To help with this, we could teach learners strategies for managing stress, building empathy, and resolving conflicts; we could use journals or discussion prompts to help learners recognise their strengths and set personal goals; and we could help learners focus on the positive aspects of their lives and the contributions of others.

Learners are more likely to believe in themselves when they see others, especially those they can relate to, succeeding. As such, we might introduce learners to a range of individuals who have overcome challenges to achieve success, share narratives that highlight resilience, determination, and growth, and encourage learners to inspire and uplift one another through teamwork and shared achievements.

Low self-esteem often stems from negative experiences or feelings of failure. Schools can help learners rebuild confidence by providing targeted support such as pairing learners with a trusted adult or older peer who can offer guidance and encouragement, ensuring learners have access to trained professionals who can help them address deeper emotional barriers, and working with learners to identify achievable goals and map out steps to success.

Learners are more likely to feel capable when they experience success in their learning. This can be achieved if we: Tailor teaching to meet the needs of individual learners, ensuring they can achieve meaningful progress; incorporate hands-on activities, group work, and creative projects to make learning enjoyable and rewarding; and highlight how far learners have come, no matter their starting point.

A child's self-esteem is often influenced by their interactions with peers. Schools can play a role in fostering positive relationships, including by using activities like circle time to discuss the importance of treating others well; taking a zero-tolerance approach to behaviours that harm learners' sense of safety and self-worth, and using group work and team sports to help learners build supportive friendships.

Finally, parents and families play a key role in shaping children's self-esteem. Schools can support families to nurture confidence at home, including by regularly communicating with families about their child's achievements, no matter how small, as well as offering guidance on how parents can build their child's self-esteem through encouragement and positive reinforcement, and by working together with families to address challenges and celebrate progress.

Self-evaluation

Here are five self-evaluation questions to consider before you move on:

1. How effectively do you think the strategies outlined for building learner confidence could be implemented in your own classroom? Can you identify any potential challenges or barriers to their application?

2. What specific methods mentioned in this chapter (e.g., setting high expectations, teaching resilience, promoting peer relationships) have you already used, and how have they impacted your learners' confidence and self-esteem?

3. In what ways do you plan to integrate the ideas on fostering a growth mindset and creating a culture of belonging into your teaching practices, and how will you measure their success?

4. How do you currently support disadvantaged learners in your setting, and what additional steps can you take to enhance their sense of belonging, empowerment, and confidence according to the suggestions in this chapter?

5. Reflecting on your own approach to fostering self-esteem in learners, how can you ensure that you consistently model and encourage confidence-building behaviours, both in individual interactions and group settings?

17 Reading for pleasure

Reading for pleasure is not merely a leisurely pastime; it is a cornerstone of lifelong learning and personal growth. Unlike the mandated reading tasks of school curriculums, where texts are often dissected for meaning and analysis, reading for pleasure invites an intrinsic, self-motivated engagement with stories, ideas, and knowledge. This distinction is crucial, for it is through this voluntary immersion that we unlock a host of benefits that extend far beyond the pages of a book.

As I explained in *The Stories We Tell*,[1] stories help give meaning to our lives:

Before the invention of writing, people told each other stories as a means of passing important information from branch to branch down the family tree, and stories have long been used as a conduit to convey a society's values, morals, and customs. In fact, storytelling has played an important role in every society throughout history. In ancient Greece, for example, storytelling was integral to the culture, with myths and legends passed baton-like between generations. In medieval Europe, troubadours and minstrels travelled town to town, telling stories and singing songs.

The earliest forms of storytelling were likely oral traditions, whereby stories were shared through the spoken word and memorisation. But, with the invention of writing, storytelling took on new forms. Epic poems such as the Iliad *and the* Odyssey *were written down, allowing them to be preserved and more easily shared. In the Middle Ages, stories were often written down in the form of manuscripts, which were painstakingly copied by hand.*

The advent of the printing press in the 15th century enabled stories to be shared on a much larger scale, leading to the rise of the novel as a popular form of storytelling. In the 20th century, radio, television, and film provided more media for storytelling, allowing stories to be told to larger audiences and on a more epic scale.

Today, the art of storytelling continues to evolve with the rise of digital media and the internet. Social media, blogs, podcasts, short-form videos, and other types of digital content have given people new ways to share their stories with the world and have democratised storytelling, giving many more people a voice with which to tell their own tales.

> As such, despite myriad changes in technology and media – or perhaps because of it – storytelling remains a fundamental part of human culture, connecting us to each other and to our shared history.
>
> Stories give meaning to our lives and make us who we are. They shape our self-awareness, thus helping us to make sense of personal experiences, no matter how complex or difficult. Stories can also have a profound impact on our behaviours, values, and attitudes – as well as on our very belief system.

In sum, stories don't just help us make sense of ourselves; they teach us important lessons and convey complex ideas, thus helping us make sense of the world around us.

And stories help us connect with other people. When we hear a story, we often identify with the characters and their experiences, even if they are very different from our own. This connection can foster empathy and understanding, helping us appreciate different perspectives and experiences.

Reading stories for pleasure is therefore vital for helping all learners engage at school and in life and thus key to fostering a culture of inclusion and belonging. There are several key benefits to reading for pleasure:

1. *Academic outcomes*

   Studies consistently show that children who read for pleasure perform better in literacy tests and, importantly, across a range of subjects, including mathematics and science. Why? Because reading nurtures vocabulary, comprehension, and critical thinking skills. It broadens horizons, introduces new ideas, and sharpens the ability to make connections between seemingly disparate concepts – all of which underpin academic success.

2. *Emotional health and well-being*

   Books are a refuge, and act as a window and a mirror. They offer escapism, providing a window into other worlds and lives, but also reflect our own experiences, helping us to process emotions and navigate challenges. This duality is particularly vital for young readers, who are still developing their emotional literacy. Through stories, they can explore complex emotions in a safe and controlled environment.

3. *Social skills*

   Reading fiction has been shown to increase empathy. As readers delve into the lives of characters, they practice putting themselves in another's shoes, understanding different perspectives and motivations. This is not just an academic skill but a societal one, fostering compassion and cooperation in a world that often feels divided.

4. *Cultural and historical awareness*

   Books are a bridge to other cultures, times, and places. They allow readers to experience history and geography through the eyes of those who lived it, cultivating a greater appreciation for diversity. In doing so, reading for pleasure builds a sense of connection to the global community and encourages curiosity about the world.

5. *Developing lifelong habits*

The joy of reading begets more reading. A child who finds pleasure in books is more likely to carry that habit into adulthood. This creates a virtuous cycle of learning, as adults who read are better equipped to navigate the complexities of modern life, from analysing media to making informed decisions.

It's a personal pursuit but it requires a partnership

While reading for pleasure is a personal pursuit and thus is inherently self-driven, the role of schools and parents in fostering this love of books cannot be understated.

Our classrooms should brim with a variety of texts, catering to different interests and reading levels, and the school day should allow time for independent reading.

Parents and families, meanwhile, have a crucial role to play in modelling reading as a pleasurable activity and in creating a home environment rich in books and storytelling.

In a world dominated by smart screens and social media, where attention spans are constantly under siege, reading for pleasure remains a beacon of quiet contemplation and intellectual engagement. By nurturing a love for books, we can equip learners with the skills, not only to succeed academically, but also to thrive emotionally and socially.

How can we foster a culture of reading for pleasure in schools?

Reading for pleasure has been a hot topic in UK education for a few years, with the government and the inspectorate championing its importance. But creating a culture of reading for pleasure is not merely about ticking boxes or fulfilling a curriculum requirement; rather, it is about igniting a lifelong love of stories and knowledge, about helping learners discover the utter joy of losing themselves in the pages of a book.

To achieve this, we must move beyond the mechanics of literacy – important though they are – and focus instead on the magic of reading. Here are some practical strategies to embed a culture of reading for pleasure in schools:

1. *Build an inviting reading environment*

   A school that values reading should look and feel like it. Classrooms and communal areas should feature enticing book displays, comfortable reading corners, and walls adorned with book recommendations, quotes, and learners' and staff's reviews. The school library should be a hub of activity, stocked with a diverse range of books to cater for all interests and reading abilities. Importantly, the environment must signal that reading is not just encouraged but celebrated.

2. *Allocate time to read*

   If we want children to read, we must give them the time to do so. We might designate daily or weekly sessions, perhaps in tutor time, for uninterrupted independent reading, where learners can select a book of their choice and read without the pressure of analysis or assessment. Teachers, too, should model this behaviour, demonstrating that reading is a pleasurable activity for all ages.

3. *Widen the definition of reading*

   To foster a love of reading, we must value all forms of reading – novels, comics, graphic novels, magazines, blogs, and audiobooks. Recognising and celebrating a broad range of texts helps to dismantle the misconception that reading for pleasure must always involve literary classics or lengthy tomes. Every form of reading has its merits and can act as a gateway to deeper engagement with books.

4. *Create a community of readers*

   Schools thrive when they foster a sense of shared purpose, and this applies to reading, too. We might therefore establish book clubs, reading challenges, or themed book weeks to bring learners together around a shared love of stories. We might encourage older learners to act as reading mentors for younger learners, creating a ripple effect of enthusiasm and fostering peer-to-peer learning.

5. *Make reading social*

   Reading need not be a solitary activity. We might use class time to share books through read-aloud sessions, where teachers bring stories to life with expression and enthusiasm. We might organise author visits and virtual talks to inspire learners and deepen their connection to the world of books. Social activities such as these help learners see reading as something vibrant and communal.

6. *Empower choice and agency*

   One of the simplest ways to nurture a love of reading is to give learners autonomy. We should allow learners to choose their own books, rather than dictating what they must read. Of course, we should guide them with thoughtful recommendations, but we should also allow their preferences to lead the way. The more ownership they feel over their reading choices, the more engaged they will become.

7. *Involve parents and families*

   The home environment is pivotal in shaping attitudes towards reading. We can support families by sharing tips on fostering a love of books, recommending age-appropriate reads, and hosting family reading events. A strong school-home partnership reinforces the message that reading is both valuable and enjoyable.

8. *Celebrate successes, big and small*

   We should recognise and celebrate reading achievements in all forms. Whether it's completing a first book, exploring a new genre, or contributing a book review, every step in a learner's reading journey is worth acknowledging. Awards, certificates, or simple public praise can go a long way in building confidence and enthusiasm.

9. *Embed reading across the curriculum*

   Finally, we should embed reading into every aspect of school life, not just form time and English lessons. Reading should run through the school curriculum like the letters in a stick of rock. For example, history lessons could involve historical novels, science lessons might explore biographies of great scientists, and art projects can draw inspiration from illustrated books. Showing learners that reading has relevance across all disciplines reinforces its importance and appeal.

By embedding these strategies into daily school life, we can nurture a generation of confident, curious, and passionate readers. But be warned: A culture of reading for pleasure is not built overnight; rather, it takes persistence and a shared commitment. It's a war of attrition, but it's worth fighting because the true power of reading lies not, or at least not solely, in the improved academic outcomes it might secure, but in the doors it might open to imagination, understanding, and the world beyond.

Reading for pleasure and attainment

When learners engage with books out of personal interest and curiosity, rather than obligation, the impact on their academic achievement can be profound and far-reaching. The benefits of reading for pleasure extend well beyond literacy itself, influencing a wide range of cognitive, social, and emotional skills that underpin success in school and beyond.

At its core, reading for pleasure directly improves literacy skills – the very foundation of learning. Learners who read regularly develop stronger vocabularies, better comprehension, and an increased ability to decode complex texts. Importantly, they also gain fluency, which allows them to focus on meaning rather than mechanics when reading. These gains translate into more confident learners, better equipped to tackle demanding academic tasks *across all subjects*.

Indeed, research has repeatedly shown that learners who read for pleasure outperform their peers in subjects far removed from English. For instance, and as I mentioned earlier, regular reading improves mathematical and scientific reasoning skills because reading fosters critical thinking, problem-solving, and the ability to draw connections between concepts – all essential for tackling complex challenges in STEM subjects. Moreover, the ability to read and process information quickly and accurately enables learners to engage more effectively with textbooks, exam papers, and other written resources, giving them a crucial edge in assessment settings.

Furthermore, reading for pleasure builds the cognitive toolkit needed for academic attainment. Through books, learners encounter new ideas, unfamiliar perspectives, and diverse problem-solving approaches. This enriches their general knowledge, deepens their cultural awareness, and hones their analytical thinking. The breadth and depth of understanding gained from reading for pleasure cannot be overstated – it is learning in its most authentic and organic form.

Academic success is not solely about intellect; emotional resilience and social understanding play pivotal roles, too. Reading for pleasure allows learners to explore emotions, grapple with moral dilemmas, and consider alternative viewpoints through the experiences of characters. This nurtures empathy, emotional intelligence, and self-awareness – qualities that are increasingly recognised as key to success in education and life.

And then there's motivation . . .

Unlike compulsory reading tasks, which can sometimes feel like a chore, reading for pleasure is self-directed and enjoyable. This positive association with reading motivates learners to engage more frequently and for longer periods, creating a virtuous cycle of skill development and academic progress.

The benefits of reading for pleasure are particularly striking when it comes to addressing educational inequality. Studies suggest that the impact of regular reading on academic attainment can be greater than that of socio-economic background. In other words, reading for pleasure has the potential to level the playing field, offering all learners – regardless of their starting point – an opportunity to excel.

Reading for pleasure and equity

Reading for pleasure is a powerful equaliser in education. For disadvantaged learners, in particular, it provides opportunities to bridge gaps in language, knowledge, and life experiences that may exist due to socio-economic circumstances. By fostering a love of reading, schools can empower these learners with the skills and confidence needed to thrive academically, socially, and emotionally.

Disadvantaged learners often start school with lower levels of literacy and a more limited vocabulary than their peers. Reading for pleasure helps close this gap by exposing learners to a rich array of words and ideas, improving their comprehension, and building the foundations for academic success. Crucially, it nurtures the critical thinking and problem-solving skills that underpin learning across the curriculum.

Moreover, regular reading cultivates cultural capital – the knowledge and experiences that enable learners to engage confidently with the wider world. Through books, learners can explore different perspectives, gain insights into unfamiliar contexts, and develop empathy, all of which help them feel connected to a broader community.

Furthermore, for disadvantaged learners, reading can – as I've said – offer a safe escape and a means of exploring emotions in a controlled and non-judgemental space. Stories can act as mirrors, reflecting their own experiences, or as windows, offering a glimpse into other lives and possibilities. These dual functions build resilience, self-awareness, and a sense of agency, helping learners navigate the challenges they face.

And as we've seen, reading for pleasure fosters a sense of achievement. When learners finish a book or discover a story that resonates, their confidence grows, encouraging them to take on new challenges – both in reading and in life.

To unlock these benefits, we must adopt deliberate strategies to engage disadvantaged learners with reading. Here are some suggestions:

1. *Make books accessible to all*

   Access to books is a significant barrier for many disadvantaged learners. We can address this by ensuring libraries are well-stocked with diverse and engaging texts that reflect a range of cultures, backgrounds, and interests. We should consider offering books to borrow or keep and explore partnerships with local libraries or charities to extend access beyond school hours.

2. *Encourage book diversity*

   Not every learner will gravitate towards traditional novels, and many disadvantaged learners will not have access to novels at home or have been encouraged to read classic literature. We should therefore cater to diverse tastes by including comics, graphic novels, magazines, poetry, audiobooks, and non-fiction in our collection. We should validate all forms of reading because this can help learners see themselves as readers, regardless of their starting point.

3. *Foster a love of storytelling*

   For some learners, the mechanics of reading can be a source of frustration. Storytelling and shared reading sessions – where teachers or peers read aloud with expression and enthusiasm – can demonstrate the joy of stories without the pressure of decoding words. These sessions also build listening skills and model fluent reading.

4. *Build relationships through reading*

   Positive relationships with trusted adults are key to engaging disadvantaged learners. We should take the time to talk to learners about their interests and recommend books they might enjoy. By showing genuine enthusiasm for reading, adults can inspire learners to give it a try.

5. *Provide the time and space to read at school*

   Many disadvantaged learners do not have quiet, comfortable spaces to read at home. We can help by building independent reading time into the school day. This ensures every learner can engage with books in a calm and supportive setting.

6. *Engage parents and families*

   Disadvantaged learners benefit immensely when reading is reinforced at home. As I've already suggested, we should therefore provide parents and families with practical tips and resources, and organise family reading events to model reading as a shared and enjoyable activity. Offering books to take home can help make reading part of family life. Our efforts should prioritise the families of disadvantaged and vulnerable learners.

For disadvantaged learners, reading for pleasure is far more than a pastime; it is a gateway to opportunity and empowerment. By making books accessible, creating a reading-friendly culture, and fostering a genuine love of stories, schools can help these learners unlock their potential and transform their futures.

Self-evaluation

Before we continue our exploration of reading for pleasure, take a moment to reflect on what you've read so far. You might find the following self-evaluation questions useful:

1. What do you think are the primary academic benefits of reading for pleasure, and how do they extend beyond literacy skills?
2. How can reading for pleasure contribute to emotional well-being, and in what ways can it help students navigate their emotions?
3. What role does empathy play in reading fiction, and how does this benefit students' social development?
4. In your opinion, how can reading for pleasure help foster cultural and historical awareness in learners?
5. How does reading for pleasure create lifelong learning habits, and why is this important for students' future success?
6. What strategies from this chapter could you apply to create a culture of reading for pleasure in your classroom or school?
7. What is the importance of allowing students to choose their own reading material, and how does it contribute to their engagement with reading?
8. How can parents and families support a child's love of reading, and what role do they play in reinforcing the school's efforts?
9. What are some ways to make reading a more social and communal activity within a school setting?
10. How does reading for pleasure contribute to addressing educational inequality, especially for disadvantaged learners? What steps can schools take to make books more accessible to all students?

Reading for pleasure and boys

Boys are often perceived as more reluctant readers than girls, a trend supported by research showing that boys are less likely to engage with books voluntarily. Yet, reading for pleasure is especially important for boys, as it helps address the gender literacy gap, nurtures essential life skills, and provides a foundation for academic and personal success. Schools play a critical role in reversing this trend by fostering a reading culture that appeals to boys and meets their specific needs.

The gender gap in literacy is a longstanding issue, with boys frequently underperforming in reading and writing compared to girls. Reading for pleasure offers a way to bridge this divide, as it builds vocabulary, comprehension, and fluency – all vital components of literacy. Boys who read regularly are better equipped to tackle the demands of the curriculum and are more likely to excel in other subjects where reading and comprehension are crucial.

Reading also allows boys to explore emotions and relationships in a safe and controlled way. Through stories, they can encounter perspectives and situations they may not experience in their daily lives, building empathy and emotional intelligence. These skills are particularly important for boys, who may feel societal pressure to suppress emotions or avoid discussing feelings.

Additionally, when boys discover the joy of reading, it sets them on a path to lifelong learning. Books can fuel curiosity, spark creativity, and provide a means of exploring interests. By fostering a love of reading early on, schools help boys develop habits that extend beyond their formal education.

To engage boys with reading for pleasure, we should adopt targeted strategies that account for their interests and motivations. Here are some suggestions – albeit with an important caveat that we must avoid perpetuating stereotypes and seek to understand the factors at play in our schools. After all, not all boys like football!

1. Choose books that capture boys' interest

We should try to offer a wide range of books that align with boys' interests, such as action-packed adventures, sports stories, humorous tales, and non-fiction on topics like science, technology, or history. Graphic novels, comics, and audiobooks are also excellent choices, particularly for boys who may find traditional novels daunting.

2. Showcase positive role models

Boys often need to see reading as something relevant to their identity. We should therefore encourage male staff members, older learners, and community figures to act as reading role models. When boys see men they admire discussing and enjoying books, it challenges stereotypes and normalises reading as a positive activity for everyone.

3. Provide freedom of choice

Choice is key to engaging boys in reading, just as it is with disadvantaged learners. We should therefore allow boys to select books that appeal to their interests and preferences, rather than prescribing what they should read. This autonomy fosters a sense of ownership and makes reading feel personal and enjoyable.

4. Make reading active and social

Boys often thrive on activity and competition. We should therefore incorporate reading challenges, quizzes, and group discussions to add a social and interactive dimension to reading. Gamifying the reading experience, such as through reading "missions" or online reading platforms, can also capture boys' interest.

5. Recognise and celebrate achievements

Celebrating boys' reading milestones can boost their confidence and motivation. As such, we should display their book reviews, offer rewards for participation in reading activities, or create leaderboards to track progress in a fun and supportive way. Positive reinforcement helps boys see reading as a valuable and rewarding pursuit.

6. Integrate reading with other interests

It might be helpful to link reading to activities that boys already enjoy. For instance, we could connect books to sports, video games, or hobbies. We might suggest biographies of athletes, stories about teamwork, or technical guides that align with their passions. This approach helps boys see reading as relevant and exciting.

7. Involve parents and families

As was the case with disadvantaged learners, parental support is also vital in encouraging boys to read. We should therefore provide parents and families with resources and guidance on choosing books that their sons might enjoy, and emphasise the importance of creating a reading-friendly home environment. We should encourage fathers to read with their sons and to model reading for pleasure, whether that be the daily newspaper, sports and motor magazines, spy and thriller novels, or less 'gender-stereotypical' texts such as classic literature. The text type and genre is less important than the act of reading itself. We might also host family reading events to build connections between home and school reading cultures.

8. Challenge stereotypes

Finally, we should challenge the idea that reading is a passive or solitary activity. We should promote books that align with boys' perceptions of adventure, exploration, and achievement, while also exposing them to a variety of genres and styles. We should encourage discussions about books that defy traditional notions of "boys' stories".

Reading for pleasure is not just a key to closing the gender literacy gap – it is a gateway to confidence, curiosity, and success for boys. By offering targeted support, fostering positive role models, and aligning reading with boys' interests, schools can help every boy discover the joy of books.

Reading for pleasure and language and literacy

Reading for pleasure is a cornerstone of language and literacy development, playing a vital role in enhancing learners' reading, writing, and language skills. Unlike reading for academic purposes, which often focuses on analysis and comprehension, reading for pleasure allows learners to engage with texts freely and joyfully, creating an environment where literacy skills flourish naturally.

Here's how reading for pleasure drives improvements in literacy and language capability and why we must prioritise fostering a love of reading . . .

1. Vocabulary growth

One of the most immediate benefits of reading for pleasure is vocabulary acquisition.

Learners who read widely are exposed to a rich and varied range of words, including those rarely encountered in everyday conversation or classroom instruction. Books introduce learners to nuanced language, technical terms, and cultural expressions, broadening their lexical repertoire.

This expanded vocabulary not only improves reading comprehension but also enhances learners' ability to express themselves clearly and effectively in both written and spoken language.

2. Improved reading fluency

Regular reading helps learners develop fluency – the ability to read accurately, smoothly, and with proper expression. When reading for pleasure, learners engage with texts for longer periods, allowing them to practise decoding and recognising words effortlessly. This repeated exposure strengthens their ability to read quickly and confidently, freeing up cognitive resources for deeper comprehension.

Fluency, in turn, underpins success across the curriculum, enabling learners to navigate textbooks, exam papers, and other written resources with ease.

3. Better reading comprehension skills

Reading for pleasure improves comprehension by encouraging learners to engage deeply with stories and texts. Unlike assigned reading tasks, which may focus on surface-level understanding, reading for enjoyment prompts learners to infer meaning, interpret themes, and connect ideas.

This engagement fosters critical thinking and analytical skills, helping learners to decipher complex texts, evaluate arguments, and synthesise information – all essential capabilities in education and beyond.

4. Better writing composition skills

Reading and writing are intrinsically linked, with one reinforcing the other. Learners who read for pleasure develop an intuitive sense of how language works – its rhythms, structures, and conventions. By encountering a variety of writing styles and genres, they absorb lessons in sentence construction, narrative techniques, and rhetorical devices.

As a result, these learners are better equipped to craft their own writing, whether it be creative stories, persuasive essays, or analytical responses. They also develop a greater appreciation for tone, voice, and audience, key elements of effective communication.

5. Links to language acquisition

For learners learning English as an additional language (EAL) and for those developing their skills in other languages in MFL, reading for pleasure provides invaluable exposure to authentic language use. It introduces idiomatic expressions, grammatical patterns, and cultural nuances that cannot be fully captured through rote learning or isolated vocabulary exercises.

6. Improved confidence and motivation

Engaging with books they enjoy helps learners develop confidence in their reading abilities. This sense of achievement motivates them to tackle increasingly challenging texts, creating a virtuous cycle of improvement. Crucially, the positive experiences associated with reading for pleasure also reduce the anxiety that can sometimes accompany literacy tasks, fostering a growth mindset towards learning.

7. Encouraging lifelong language learning

Reading for pleasure instils habits that extend beyond the classroom. Learners who enjoy reading are more likely to continue exploring books throughout their lives, gaining ongoing access to new knowledge, ideas, and perspectives. This lifelong engagement with texts continually reinforces literacy and language skills.

Reading for pleasure is a powerful driver of literacy and language capability. By expanding vocabulary, enhancing fluency, and fostering comprehension, it equips learners with the tools they need to succeed in school and beyond. Moreover, it strengthens writing, supports language acquisition, and builds confidence, making it an essential component of any educational strategy.

When we prioritise reading for pleasure, we empower learners to unlock the full potential of literacy – opening doors to academic success, personal growth, and a lifetime of learning.

Reading for pleasure and inclusion and belonging

I'm sure it's already obvious how reading for pleasure intersects with our core themes of inclusion and belonging, but . . .

Reading for pleasure plays a crucial role in fostering a sense of inclusion and belonging within schools and communities because books have the unique power to bring people together, to amplify diverse voices, and to bridge gaps in understanding and experience. For learners from all backgrounds, reading for pleasure is not just a private activity but a communal one, offering opportunities to celebrate individuality while cultivating empathy and connection.

Here's how reading for pleasure is intricately linked to inclusion and belonging – and what we can do to harness this potential:

1. Stories as mirrors, windows . . . and doors

I've already argued that books, like our curriculum, can act as mirrors and windows, but they can also be doors . . .

Books act as **mirrors** when they reflect a reader's own experiences, affirming their identity and validating their place in the world. For learners from marginalised or underrepresented groups, seeing themselves in stories can be profoundly empowering.

Books also serve as **windows**, offering glimpses into lives and perspectives different from one's own. This helps learners develop empathy and an appreciation for diversity, laying the foundation for mutual respect and understanding.

But books can act as **doors**, too, inviting readers to step into new worlds, expand their horizons, and imagine possibilities beyond their immediate context.

2. Celebrating diversity through stories

A robust culture of reading for pleasure celebrates the richness of human diversity. By introducing learners to stories from various cultures, backgrounds, and experiences, we can help break down stereotypes and challenge bias. Reading about characters who overcome adversity, navigate complex identities, or live in different parts of the world fosters a greater understanding of the shared humanity that unites us all.

This approach also encourages learners to celebrate their own identities and those of their peers, building a school environment that values and respects everyone.

3. Building shared experiences

As I've said, reading for pleasure is not just a solitary act, it can also be deeply social. When learners read and discuss books together, they share experiences that transcend their individual differences. Stories spark conversations about values, beliefs, and emotions, creating opportunities for meaningful connection.

Group activities such as book clubs, storytelling sessions, and peer reading schemes build a sense of community and encourage learners to listen to and learn from one another. These shared experiences foster trust and mutual understanding, strengthening bonds within the school community.

4. Reducing barriers to belonging

For some learners, feelings of exclusion stem from not seeing themselves represented in school materials or being unable to access the same resources as their peers. A commitment to reading for pleasure that prioritises accessibility and inclusivity can help break down these barriers.

We can ensure that our school library and reading lists feature diverse authors, characters, and themes, making it clear that everyone belongs. We can also offer accessible formats, such as large-print books, audiobooks, and texts for learners with additional learning needs, ensuring that all learners can engage with reading.

5. Promoting empathy and understanding

Reading for pleasure helps learners to step into others' shoes and view the world from different perspectives. This is especially important in a diverse school community, where learners may encounter peers whose lives and experiences differ significantly from their own.

Through stories, learners learn to navigate complex emotions and social dynamics, cultivating empathy and respect. This not only improves relationships among peers but also contributes to a more inclusive and harmonious school culture.

6. Encouraging self-expression and voice

Reading for pleasure inspires creativity and self-expression. By exploring different genres and styles, learners are encouraged to share their own stories, helping them find and celebrate their unique voices. Schools that celebrate these voices – through creative writing, drama, or storytelling – create spaces where every learner feels seen, heard, and valued.

To harness the power of reading for pleasure in promoting inclusion and belonging, we might also adopt the following strategies:

- **Diversify reading materials**: Curate a library that reflects the diversity of the school community and the wider world. We can include books by authors from underrepresented backgrounds and stories featuring a range of identities and experiences.

- **Celebrate cultural literacy**: Host events like multicultural book fairs or themed reading weeks that highlight stories from different traditions and perspectives
- **Encourage group reading activities**: Create opportunities for learners to share books and stories, whether through book clubs, paired reading schemes, or collaborative storytelling sessions
- **Provide access for all**: Ensure that all learners, regardless of ability or background, can access books in formats that meet their needs
- **Model inclusive reading practices**: Teachers and staff should model inclusive behaviours by reading and discussing diverse books, demonstrating that all stories are valuable.
- **Foster peer recommendation**: Encourage learners to recommend books to one another, creating a culture where they feel confident sharing their preferences and insights
- **Link stories to values**: Use books as a springboard for discussing themes like kindness, respect, and justice, embedding inclusion into the broader curriculum

Self-evaluation

Take a moment to further reflect on reading for pleasure and answer these questions:

1. How does this chapter explain the importance of reading for pleasure in addressing the gender literacy gap, particularly for boys?
2. What strategies does this chapter suggest to engage boys in reading for pleasure? Which ones do you find most effective, and why?
3. How do you think reading for pleasure enhances vocabulary and reading fluency?
4. Reading for pleasure boosts writing skills. How do you think it helps with writing composition and creativity?
5. What role does reading for pleasure play in fostering empathy and emotional intelligence in boys? Can you think of any examples where this might apply in real life?
6. There is a link between reading for pleasure and inclusion. How can books act as "mirrors" and "windows" for readers?
7. Which suggestions in this chapter do you think would help create a more inclusive and welcoming reading environment for all learners, including those from marginalised backgrounds?

8. How does the concept of reading for pleasure as a social activity (e.g., group discussions, book clubs) enhance the experience?

9. This chapter advocates for parental involvement in promoting reading for pleasure. In what ways can schools and families collaborate to encourage this habit in boys?

10. What is your personal takeaway from this text about the relationship between reading for pleasure, language development, and lifelong learning?

Note

1 Bromley, M. (2024) *The stories we tell*. Oxford: Routledge.

PART FIVE
Putting it into practice

18 Action planning

Equality, diversity, and inclusion are often assumed to be synonymous, but the distinct meanings of each of these three words are well worthy of dissection . . .

E is for equality – this means ensuring everyone has the same opportunities, removing barriers that prevent individuals from achieving their potential. Crucially, this does not mean treating everyone identically but rather equitably, accounting for different needs.

D is for diversity – this means celebrating the differences between people, recognising and valuing the varied backgrounds, identities, and perspectives that enrich a learning community.

I is for inclusion – this goes a step further, ensuring that diverse individuals feel welcomed, valued, and respected, and are able to participate fully in school life and are helped to prepare for full and active participation in wider society, both now and as adults.

To embed these three principles in our schools, we must first understand why some learners sometimes feel excluded. Feeling excluded, different, or *other*-ed stems from a combination of factors, including though not limited to systemic barriers, social barriers, and practical barriers. To help, we need to embed EDI in policy and practice, empower staff and learners, celebrate diversity, and prioritise well-being and accessibility.

Whatever strategies we deploy, to be a truly inclusive school, we must continually assess our practices by auditing three sets of factors: 1 School-based factors, such as representation, environment, and engagement; 2 Home-based factors, such as parental involvement, digital access, and support networks; and 3 Learner-based factors, such as belonging, engagement, and achievement.

My 3Cs of inclusion are:

1. ***Culture***: In an inclusive culture, every member of the school community is made to feel welcome and treats one another with dignity and respect.

2. **Collaboration**: Inclusive schools believe in collaboration over competition, they foster a sense of community, or team spirit, and of shared endeavour – working together towards a common goal, sharing success and failure.

3. **Curriculum**: In inclusive schools, teaching is planned with the learning of all learners in mind. Lessons encourage the participation of all learners. Learners are actively involved in their own learning, and they learn collaboratively. Assessment contributes to the achievements of all learners.

So, what does this look like in practice? Let's pull together all the advice contained in this book and draft an action plan.

Step 1: Focus on three areas of professional practice

1. **Planning**: An inclusive curriculum is one that reflects, celebrates, and supports the diverse experiences of all learners. It acknowledges the richness of the communities we serve while equipping learners with the knowledge and skills they need to thrive in an interconnected world. Achieving this requires a deliberate approach to curriculum design, ensuring that every learner feels seen, valued, and empowered.

In practice, this means:

- Reflect: Ensure the curriculum is a mirror, reflecting the lived experiences of learners

- Reveal: Ensure the curriculum is a window, revealing a life, or lives, beyond learners' own lived experiences, exposing them to the diversity and richness of the wider world

- Review: Ensure the curriculum meets the needs of all learners, is regularly reviewed and adapted

2. **Teaching**: Inclusive teaching is about ensuring that every learner, regardless of their background, ability, or starting point, can access and benefit from the same ambitious curriculum. Inclusive teaching involves balancing high expectations of all with thoughtful support for those who need it when they need it, ensuring that all learners feel valued and empowered to succeed.

In practice, this means:

- Diagnose: Understand the individual starting points and additional needs of our learners; use diagnostic assessments and start by identifying what learners already know and what gaps need to be addressed

- Deliver: Provide the support necessary for all learners to engage with the same challenging and meaningful content. We should set high expectations for everyone and believe that every learner can achieve success.

- Differentiate: Be flexible and responsive in the moment, as well as planning ahead to meet diverse needs. We should regularly check for understanding during lessons and adjust teaching based on what learners demonstrate they know and can do.

3. *Assessment*: Assessments – when done well – can provide crucial insights into what learners know and can do. However, to be truly effective, assessments must be inclusive – designed and delivered in such a way that allows all learners, regardless of their needs or circumstances, to demonstrate their learning and progress.

In practice, this means:

- Accessibility: Ensure all learners can engage with the process. Use plain language and avoid unnecessary jargon. Present information in a variety of ways to accommodate different learning preferences and needs. Ensure time allocations reflect the complexity of the task, accounting for processing or mobility challenges. Minimise external stressors such as noise, distractions, or unclear rules, and provide a calm, structured setting.

- Adjustments: Reasonable adjustments enable learners to demonstrate their learning without being unfairly hindered by barriers unrelated to the knowledge or skills being tested. Allow learners to choose how they present their knowledge, whether through essays, presentations, diagrams, or practical demonstrations.

- Assistive technologies: Use software such as speech-to-text, spell checkers, and grammar tools to help learners with language processing challenges express their ideas more effectively. Customise digital assessments to suit individual needs, such as altering font sizes, colours, or line spacing. Use tools such as calculators, concept-mapping software, or prompts to help learners focus on the key learning objectives.

Step 2: Mind the gaps

To achieve inclusion and belonging, we need to understand who is not yet included in school life and who does not yet feel as if they belong in our classroom.

In practice, we need to focus on:

1. *The gender gap*

    - Understand the causes: Biological factors such as developmental differences and neurological variations; environmental factors such as cultural expectations; school environment; role models and representation; stereotypes and bias; engagement with reading

    - Take a multi-faceted approach: Diversify teaching methods and adopt a range of pedagogical styles; promote literacy for boys and encourage reading; challenge gender stereotypes; ensure there are more male role models in education;

provide behaviour support programmes, tailored interventions designed to help reduce classroom disruption and exclusion rates among boys; rethink assessments and ensure a greater balance is struck between classwork and exams

- Understand how the gender gap intersects with inclusion and belonging and foster a welcoming environment, provide more role models, adapt the curriculum, tailor teaching strategies, offer mentorship and peer support, and provide staff training

2. **The ethnicity gap**

- Understand that it's intersectional with overlapping factors including: Socio-economic disadvantage; language barriers; systemic bias and low expectations; lack of representation; parental engagement; and peer dynamics

- Address the root causes and tailor interventions including: Targeted support for disadvantaged learners; anti-bias training for teachers; culturally inclusive curriculum; improving representation in the workforce; parental engagement programmes; challenging stereotypes; mentorship and peer support

- Understand how the ethnicity gap intersects with inclusion and belonging and create a culturally inclusive curriculum, train staff to recognise and challenge bias, actively celebrate diversity, encourage diverse leadership and role models, build stronger links with families by offering language support and tailored workshops for parents, and tackle racism proactively by implementing clear anti-racism policies

3. **The SEND gap**

- Understand interrelated factors impacting on SEND including: Delayed identification and support; inadequate resources; mainstream inclusion challenges; exclusion rates; low expectations and bias; transitions and continuity

- Understand how the SEND gap intersects with inclusion and belonging, including classroom integration, peer relationships, teacher attitudes and expectations, accessibility and adaptations, and parental and learner voice, then: Adopt inclusive teaching practices, such as adaptive or responsive teaching including the use of task-scaffolding; cultivate an inclusive school culture, such as by celebrating diversity and promoting awareness and understanding of SEND; provide emotional and social support, such as creating safe spaces; enhance accessibility by investing in assistive technologies; involve families and learners in decision-making

4. **The socio-economic gap**

- Investigate reasons for the socio-economic gap's existence in your school, including: Material poverty; parental engagement; school resources; gaps in cultural capital; and aspirations and motivation

Action planning

- Tackle the gap by: Ensuring that funding is used strategically to invest in evidence-based interventions; providing early intervention; investing in high-quality teaching for all; addressing the broader challenges faced by disadvantaged learners by investing in mental health and well-being services; providing all learners with opportunities to experience cultural enrichment; offering workshops or resources that help parents understand how to support their child's learning at home; and exposing learners to a wide range of careers and higher education opportunities through trips, careers fairs, and talks from relatable role models

- Understand how the socio-economic hap intersects with inclusion and belonging and build positive relationships, create an inclusive curriculum, remove economic, combat stigma, celebrate diversity, and engage families

5. **The vulnerable children gap**

    - Understand the causes of the vulnerable children gap, including: Many looked after children experience instability, such as frequent changes in foster placements or residential homes; children in care are more likely to have experienced abuse, neglect, or family breakdown; vulnerable children often lack the stable and supportive relationships that many of their peers take for granted; there is sometimes an unconscious bias among educators, social workers, or carers that leads to lower expectations for looked after and vulnerable children; frequent school moves, lack of access to resources like books or technology, and disruptions caused by court appearances or social work meetings can all detract from their ability to keep up academically.

    - Tackle the gap by: Providing stable schooling; ensuring high-quality teaching; appointing designated teachers; providing emotional and pastoral support; raising expectations and aspirations; enhancing collaboration; and monitoring and support attendance

    - Understand how the vulnerable children gap intersects with inclusion and belonging and build positive, trusting relationships to help these children feel valued, create a welcoming environment so that vulnerable children are fully integrated into school life, adapt the curriculum to reflect diverse experiences and perspectives, tackle stigma, involve learners in decision-making to foster a sense of ownership and belonging

5. **The mobility gap**

    - Understand why highly mobile learners perform worse at school, including the following factors: Service children and highly mobile learners often move between schools multiple times during their education; service children often face stress or anxiety due to parental deployment, family separation, or concerns for their parents' safety; vulnerable children often lose access to tailored support when they move schools; and frequent moves can also lead to gaps or delays in transferring school records, making it harder for teachers to understand and meet a child's needs.

- Explore solutions for closing the gap, including by: Providing more continuity in learning; enhancing transition support; tracking and sharing data; providing emotional and pastoral support; fostering a sense of belonging; raising awareness among staff; supporting families

- Understand how the mobility gap intersects with inclusion and belonging and then implement robust induction processes to help new learners settle in quickly, establish peer mentoring schemes or support groups, adapt teaching methods to accommodate mobile learners, encourage group work and collaborative projects to help foster friendships and inclusion, incorporate lessons or activities that acknowledge and celebrate the backgrounds of service children and other mobile learners, provide access to counselling or pastoral care for those service children who face emotional stress, give all staff training to help them identify signs of emotional distress and intervene early, actively involve families in the school community, and maintain strong communication during deployment periods to help parents stay connected to their children's education

Step 3: Unpack school-based causes of attainment gaps

In practice, explore:

1. Parental engagement and expectations
2. School leadership and the quality of teaching
3. School resources and infrastructure
4. Teacher perception and bias
5. Transition points
6. Social and emotional well-being

Then consider these critical enablers: Leadership; whole-school approach; teacher skills; support systems; planning time; and parental involvement.

Seek to mitigate common barriers to inclusion including: Class sizes; resources; negative attitudes; and physical barriers.

Step 4: Ensure the curriculum is inclusive

In practice, ensure lesson plans achieve:

1 Cross-curricular connections

2 Classroom consistency

3 Connections to the real world

Then ensure teaching is inclusive by moving from differentiation to adaptive teaching which is marked by: Delivering the same ambitious curriculum to all; giving the same tasks to all; having the same high expectations of all; giving the same demanding feedback to all; ensuring the same level of challenge for all; and using task scaffolds – temporary support structures – to make all this accessible.

Make use of live adaptations in response to ongoing formative assessment and/or learner observation, and planned adaptations given to those learners with known needs.

Provide task scaffolds which are visual, verbal, and written.

Know when to make these adjustments and when to scale them back by utilising ongoing low-stakes formative assessments and by considering four challenge variables: the intrinsic demand of the task, cognitive load, prior knowledge, and external support.

Then increase or decrease the challenge by sequencing learning to make the bigger picture explicit; adapting and chunking the number of things a learner has to think about; activating prior knowledge through retrieval practice immediately before the task is begun; and scaffolding for memory demands.

Finally, ensure assessment is inclusive by considering: Cultural capital bias; language barriers; socio-economic disparities; special educational needs and disabilities (SEND); gender stereotypes; and the over-emphasis on one type of intelligence.

Make assessment more inclusive by: Diversifying assessment formats; providing adjustments for SEND learners; ensuring cultural relevance; reducing the role of high-stakes testing; offering support for EAL learners; addressing socioeconomic barriers; challenging gender stereotypes; and involving learners in the process.

Step 5: Make reasonable adjustments

- When making reasonable adjustments, consider factors such as the specific needs of the learner, the resources and size of the school, health and safety implications, the practicality and effectiveness of the adjustment, and the impact on maintaining academic and extracurricular standards.

- Include adjustments such as a timetable adjustment that allows learners with learning difficulties to receive extra support without missing core lessons, a seating plan adjustment to ensure a learner with a hearing impairment is located near the teacher to aid lip-reading and hearing, flexible uniform rules to accommodate sensory needs or medical conditions, and alternative sanctions to replace exclusions when behaviour stems from a disability.

- Accept that inclusion isn't just about academic adjustments, it's about the whole school experience. As such, consider if: Extracurricular activities are accessible to learners with additional needs; events like school fairs or discos include provisions for all learners; junior leadership opportunities are open to diverse groups of learners; and learners with additional needs are active participants in representing the school.

Step 6: Use oracy as a path to inclusion

- Understand oracy's importance for educational outcomes, social mobility, preparation for the future, and civic participation.

- Explore the reasons affluent children are more confident and articulate, including a wealth of early experiences, language-rich environments, social confidence and self-belief, familiarity with formal contexts, networks and role models, and the hidden curriculum of social class.

- Then tackle the oracy gap by: Prioritising oracy across the curriculum; building social confidence through exposure; developing self-belief and growth mindsets; teaching code-switching skills; providing opportunities for leadership; ensuring fair access to opportunities; and fostering critical thinking and independence.

- Use oracy as a road to equity by: Teaching code-switching to enable learners to speak appropriately and with confidence in a range of situations; teaching debating skills to enable learners to engage in discussions and articulate their views with diplomacy; teaching rhetoric and prosody to enable learners to speak convincingly and powerfully to argue their views; teaching storytelling techniques to enable learners to narrate their own lives and the lives of others; and deploying dialogic teaching and modelling in the classroom to make oracy an integral part of the curriculum.

Step 7: Foster a culture of reading for pleasure

- Appreciate the key benefits to reading for pleasure: Academic outcomes; emotional health and well-being; social skills; cultural and historical awareness; and developing lifelong habits.

- Move beyond the mechanics of literacy and focus on the magic of reading, by building an inviting reading environment, allocating time to read, widening the definition of reading, creating a community of readers, making reading social, empowering choice and agency, involving parents and families, celebrating successes, big and small, and embedding reading across the curriculum.

- Adopt deliberate strategies to engage disadvantaged learners with reading by: Making books accessible to all; encouraging book diversity; fostering a love of storytelling; building relationships through reading; providing the time and space to read at school; and engaging parents and families.

- Engage boys with reading for pleasure by adopt targeted strategies that account for their interests and motivations and by choosing books that capture boys' interest, showcasing positive role models, providing freedom of choice, making reading active and social, recognising and celebrating achievements, integrating reading with other interests, involving parents and families, and challenging stereotypes.

- Use reading for pleasure to drive improvements in literacy and language capability including vocabulary growth, improved reading fluency, better reading comprehension skills, better writing composition skills, links to language acquisition, improved confidence and motivation, and a love of lifelong language learning.

- Use reading for pleasure to foster inclusion and belonging by: Using stories as mirrors, windows, and doors; celebrating diversity through stories; building shared experiences; reducing barriers to belonging; promoting empathy and understanding; and encouraging self-expression and voice.

Table 18.1 Embedding inclusion in your school

Objectives	Current strengths	Areas for improvement	Actions required with timescales	Success criteria
Inclusive planning				
1. To ensure curriculum plans reflect learners' lived experiences, mirroring their own lives and making them feel seen, heard, and included in school-life.				
2. To ensure curriculum plans reveal lives beyond learners' lived experiences, exposing them to the diversity and richness of the wider world.				
3. To ensure curriculum plans are regularly reviewed and adapted to meets the needs of all learners.				
4. To ensure curriculum plans include cross-curricular connections, allow for classroom consistency, and make natural connections to the real world.				
Inclusive teaching				
5. To ensure individual starting points and additional needs are diagnosed and that teachers routinely identify what learners already know and what gaps need to be addressed.				
6. To ensure that disadvantaged learners and those with additional needs are helped – through adaptive teaching techniques – to engage with the same challenging and meaningful content as their peers; to ensure teachers have the same high expectations of every learner.				
7. To ensure teachers are flexible and responsive in the moment, as well as planning ahead to meet diverse needs; to ensure teachers regularly check for understanding during lessons and adjust teaching based on what learners know and can do.				
8. To adapt teaching by: Delivering the same ambitious curriculum to all; giving the same tasks to all; having the same high expectations of all; giving the same demanding feedback to all; ensuring the same level of challenge for all; and using task scaffolds – temporary support structures – to make all this accessible.				

Action planning

	Inclusive assessment								
9. To ensure all learners can engage with assessments by: Using plain language and avoiding unnecessary jargon; presenting information in a variety of ways to accommodate different learning preferences and needs; ensuring time allocations reflect the complexity of the task, accounting for processing or mobility challenges; and minimising external stressors such as noise, distractions, or unclear rules, and providing a calm, structured setting.									
10. To make reasonable adjustments to enable learners to demonstrate their learning without being unfairly hindered by barriers unrelated to the knowledge or skills being tested.									
11. To use software to help learners with language processing challenges express their ideas more effectively; to customise digital assessments to suit individual needs; and to use tools such as calculators, concept-mapping software, or prompts to help learners focus on the key learning objectives.									
12. To design assessments that mitigate cultural capital bias, language barriers, socio-economic disparities, SEND, gender stereotypes, and the over-emphasis on one type of intelligence.									
	Oracy								
13. To tackle the oracy gap by: Prioritising oracy across the curriculum; building social confidence through exposure; developing self-belief and growth mindsets; teaching code-switching skills; providing opportunities for leadership; ensuring fair access to opportunities; and fostering critical thinking and independence.									
14. To use oracy as a road to equity by: Teaching code-switching to enable learners to speak appropriately and with confidence in a range of situations; teaching debating skills to enable learners to engage in discussions and articulate their views with diplomacy; and teaching rhetoric and prosody to enable learners to speak convincingly and powerfully to argue their views.									
15. To teach storytelling techniques to enable learners to narrate their own lives and the lives of others; to deploy dialogic teaching and modelling in the classroom to make oracy an integral part of the curriculum.									

(*Continued*)

Table 18.1 (Continued)

Objectives	Current strengths	Areas for improvement	Actions required with timescales	Success criteria
Reading for pleasure				
16. To adopt deliberate strategies to engage disadvantaged learners with reading by: Making books accessible to all; encouraging book diversity; fostering a love of storytelling; building relationships through reading; providing the time and space to read at school; and engaging parents and families.				
17. To engage boys with reading for pleasure by adopting targeted strategies that account for their interests and motivations, showcasing positive role models, providing freedom of choice, making reading active and social, recognising achievements, integrating reading with other interests, and involving parents and families.				
18. To use reading for pleasure to drive improvements in literacy and language capability including vocabulary growth, improved reading fluency, better reading comprehension skills, better writing composition skills, links to language acquisition, improved confidence and motivation, and a love of lifelong language learning.				
19. To use reading for pleasure to foster inclusion and belonging by: Celebrating diversity through stories; building shared experiences; reducing barriers to belonging; promoting empathy and understanding; and encouraging self-expression and voice.				
Holistic inclusion				
20. To ensure that inclusion isn't just about academic adjustments but also encompasses the whole school experience. Consider if: Extracurricular activities are accessible to learners with additional needs; events like school fairs or discos include provisions for all learners; junior leadership opportunities are open to diverse groups of learners; and learners with additional needs are active participants in representing the school.				

Index

accessibility 34
adaptive teaching 5, 96–103
ADHD 35, 121
assistive technology 35
attainment gaps 3

barriers to EDI 23
belonging 19

child protection plans 64
classroom consistency 4, 91
code-switching 6, 20, 130, 135–138
cognition and learning needs 5, 116
cognitive load 4, 100–103
collaboration 27
communication and interaction needs 5, 117
confidence, self-esteem 163–168
connections to the real world 4, 93
COVID 1, 58, 65
cross-curricular connections 4, 87
cultural capital (inc. cultural capital bias) 1, 19, 94, 104, 107–108
culture 27
curriculum 28
curriculum review 31

debating 6, 138–142
diagnostic assessment 31
dialogic teaching 6, 157–163
differentiation 5, 18
disciplinary literary 5
dyslexia 34

early intervention 18
EDI strategies 25
education health and care plans (EHCP) 52–54, 118
English as an additional language (EAL) 5, 106
Equality Act 2010 99, 115
equality, diversity, and inclusion (EDI) 2, 3, 22
ethnicity gap 3, 46–51

gender gap 3, 39–45

inclusive assessment 33, 104–114
inclusive planning 29, 97–95
inclusive teaching 31, 96–103
initial teacher training and early career framework (ITTECF) 96
intrinsic motivation 2

lived experiences 1, 29

marking and feedback 2
metacognition and self-regulation 2
mobility gap 3, 70–75

oracy 2, 5, 6, 20, 125–133, 134

personal education plans (PEP) 65–69
physical and sensory needs 5, 117
pomodoro Technique 16

prosody 6, 142–154
pupil premium grant 59

reading and boys 177
reading for pleasure 2, 5, 6, 20, 169
reasonable adjustments 2, 34
responsible inclusion 7
rhetoric 6, 142–154

SEND Code of Practice 28, 53
SEND gap 3, 52–57
Service Pupil Premium (SPP) 71

social, emotional, and mental health needs (SEMH) 5, 117
socio-economic gap 3, 58–63
The Stories We Tell 169–170
storytelling 6, 154–157
study skills and revision 2

task scaffolding 5, 20, 33, 98–103
teachers standards 96
transition 18

vulnerable children gap 3, 64–69

For Product Safety Concerns and Information please contact our EU representative GPSR@taylorandfrancis.com
Taylor & Francis Verlag GmbH, Kaufingerstraße 24, 80331 München, Germany

www.ingramcontent.com/pod-product-compliance
Lightning Source LLC
Chambersburg PA
CBHW062138160426
43191CB00014B/2315